**Berlitz**®

P9-AOH-070

# Croatian

phrase book & dictionary

**Berlitz Publishing**
**New York   London   Singapore**

7/14  491.82
KK   B

No part of this book may be reproduced, stored in a retrieval system or transmitted in any form or means electronic, mechanical, photocopying, recording or otherwise, without prior written permission from APA Publications.

**Contacting the Editors**
Every effort has been made to provide accurate information in this publication, but changes are inevitable. The publisher cannot be responsible for any resulting loss, inconvenience or injury. We would appreciate it if readers would call our attention to any errors or outdated information. We also welcome your suggestions; if you come across a relevant expression not in our phrase book, please contact us at: **comments@berlitzpublishing.com**

All Rights Reserved
© 2007 Berlitz Publishing/APA Publications (UK) Ltd.
Berlitz Trademark Reg. U.S. Patent Office and other countries. Marca Registrada. Used under license from Berlitz Investment Corporation.

**3rd Edition:** August 2013
Printed by CTPS in China

**Head of Language:** Kate Drynan
**Translation:** updated by Wordbank
**Design:** Beverley Speight
**Production Manager:** Vicky Glover
**Picture Researcher:** Beverley Speight
**Cover Photo:** © APA Julian Love

**Interior Photos:** APA Corrie Wingate p12, 29, 35, 37, 56, 59, 60, 64, 67, 68, 69, 71, 72, 73, 74, 75, 76, 77, 80, 82, 83, 85, 86, 87, 88, 89, 90, 91, 92, 93, 94, 95, 96, 97, 98, 99, 100, 103, 108, 110, 114, 116, 125, 127, 129, 132, 135, 139, 140; istockphoto p.1, 14, 16, 25, 32, 42, 45, 48, 63, 65, 78, 104, 119, 121, 145, 147, 148, 153, 154, 157, 159, 161; APA Mina Patria p.22; APA Britta Jaschinski p.81; APA Greg Gladman p.123; APA Bev Speight p175.

# Contents

## Food & Drink

## People

## Leisure Time

## Special Requirements

## In an Emergency

## Dictionary

# Pronunciation

This section is designed to make you familiar with the sounds of Croatian using our simplified phonetic transcription. You'll find the pronunciation of the Croatian letters and sounds explained below, together with their "imitated" equivalents. This system is used throughout the phrase book; simply read the pronunciation as if it were English, noting any special rules below.

Croatian is a Slavic language spoken by around 5 million people. It can also be understood in other republics of former Yugoslavia (Serbia, Bosnia and Herzegovina and Montenegro).

Croatian uses the Latin alphabet and spelling is largely phonetic meaning that most words are written exactly as they are pronounced, and there is a good correlation of sound to spelling. Note that any words starting with a capital letter in the middle of a sentence indicate that this word should be stressed. Single syllable words are not stressed, with the exception of the word **ne** *neh*, which, when in front of a verb, indicates negation. In practice, the second-last or third-last syllable is almost always stressed.

## Consonants

| Letter | Approximate Pronunciation | Symbol | Example | Pronunciation |
|--------|---------------------------|--------|---------|---------------|
| **cc** | like ts in lots | ts | **carina** | *tsah·rih·nah* |
| **č** | like ch in cheese, but harder | ch | **čamac** | *chah·mahts* |
| **ć** | like ch in cheese, but softer | ch | **noć** | *nohch* |
| **dž** | like j in John, but harder | j | **džem** | *jehm* |
| **đ** | like j in John, but softer | j | **đon** | *john* |
| **g** | like the g in good | g | **grad** | *grahd* |

| | | | | |
|---|---|---|---|---|
| **h** | like the h in house | h | **hitno** | *hih·tnoh* |
| **j** | like the y in yellow | y | **jutro** | *yoo·troh* |
| **lj** | a fast pronunciation of l and y | ly | **ljudi** | *lyoo·dih* |
| **nj** | like ni in onion | ny | **dinja** | *dih·nyah* |
| **r** | always trilled | r | **ruksak** | *rook·sahk* |
| **š** | like sh in short | sh | **šator** | *shah·tohr* |
| **ž** | like s in measure | zh | **žut** | *zhoot* |

Letters b, c, f, h, k, l, m, n, p, q, t, x, y, z are generally pronounced as in English.

## Vowels

| Letter | Approximate Pronunciation | Symbol | Example | Pronunciation |
|---|---|---|---|---|
| **a** | like a in father | ah | **dan** | *dahn* |
| **e** | like e in get | eh | **petak** | *peh·tahk* |
| **i** | 1. like i in sit | 1. ih | **1. ime** | *1. ih·meh* |
| | 2. like ee in meet | 2. ee | **2. pismo** | *2. pee·smoh* |
| **o** | like o in rope | oh | **more** | *moh·reh* |
| **u** | like oo in soon | oo | **sunce** | *soon·tseh* |

Croatian is a southern variant of the Slavonic languages, including Serbian, Bosnian and Slovene. Croatian and Serbian are quite similar and both languages share many pronouns and cases, and they are mutually understandable. There are however some differences in vocabulary and syntax. As a result of the Balkan conflict, the different national groups established their own official languages, and the term Croatian is now used to describe the official language of Croatia (the language used to be referred to as Serbo-Croat). An estimated five million people speak Croatian in Croatia. However, approximately 21 million people throughout the world speak a variation of the formerly shared Serbo-Croat language.

# How to use this Book

Sometimes you see two alternatives separated by a slash. Choose the one that's right for your situation.

## ESSENTIAL

| | |
|---|---|
| I'm on vacation/ business. | **Na odmoru/poslu sam.** *nah ohd·moh·roo/poh·sloo sahm* |
| I'm going to... | **Idem u...** *ih·dehm oo...* |
| I'm staying at the...Hotel. | **Odsjeo** *m*/**Odsjela** *f* **sam u hotelu...** *ohd·syeh·oh/ohd·syeh·lah sahm oo hoh·teh·loo...* |

Words you may see are shown in YOU MAY SEE boxes.

## YOU MAY SEE...

| | |
|---|---|
| **PERONI** | platforms |
| **INFORMACIJE** | information |
| **REZERVACIJE** | reservations |

Any of the words or phrases listed can be plugged into the sentence below.

## Tickets

| | |
|---|---|
| A...ticket. | **Jednu kartu...** *yeh·dnoo kahr·too...* |
| one-way | **u jednom smjeru** *oo yeh·dnohm smyeh·roo* |
| round-trip [return] | **povratnu** *poh·vrah·tnoo* |
| first class | **za prvu klasu** *zah prvoo klah·soo* |
| business class | **za biznis klasu** *zah bihz·nihs klah·soo* |
| economy class | **za ekonomsku klasu** *zah eh·koh·nohm·skooklah·soo* |

Croatian phrases appear in purple.

Read the simplified pronunciation as if it were English. For more on pronunciation, see page 7.

## The Dating Game

Where would you like to go?

I'd like to go to...

Do you like...?

**Gdje želite ići?**
*gdyeh zheh-lih-teh ih-chih*

**Htio *m*/Htjela *f* bih ići...**
*htih-oh/htyeh-lah bih ih-chih...*

**Sviđa li Vam se...?** *svih-jah lih vahm seh...*

For Communications, see page 49.

Related phrases can be found by going to the page number indicated.

When different gender forms apply, the masculine form is followed by *m*; feminine by *f*

There are two forms for "you" in Croatian. The informal forms **ti** (singular) or **vi** (plural) are used when talking to friends, relatives and among young people. The **Vi** (polite/plural) form for "you" is used when speaking to one or more persons in a formal setting.

Information boxes contain relevant country, culture and language tips.

Expressions you may hear are shown in You May Hear boxes.

## YOU MAY HEAR...

**Imate nešto za prijaviti?**
*ih-mah-teh neh-shtoh zah prih-yah-vih-tih*

Anything to declare?

Color-coded side bars identify each section of the book.

# Survival

## ESSENTIAL

I'm here on vacation [holiday]/business.
**Na odmoru/poslu sam**
*nah ohd·moh·roo/poh·sloo sahm*

I'm going to...
**Idem u...** *ih·dehm oo...*

I'm staying at the...Hotel.
**Odsjeo m/Odsjela f sam u hotelu...**
*ohd·syeh·oh/ohd·syeh·lah sahm oo hoh·teh·loo...*

## YOU MAY HEAR...

**Vašu putovnicu, molim Vas.**
*vah·shoo poo·toh·vnih·tsoo moh·lihm vahs*
Your passport, please.

**U koju svrhu ste u posjeti?**
*oo koh·yoo svr·hoo steh oo poh·syeh·tih*
What's the purpose of your visit?

**Gdje ćete odsjesti?** *gdyeh cheh·teh ohd·syeh·stih*
Where are you staying?

**Koliko ostajete?**
*koh·lih·koh ohs·tah·yeh·teh*
How long are you staying?

**S kim ste ovdje?** *skeem steh ohv·dyeh*
Who are you here with?

## Border Control

I'm just passing through.
**Samo sam u prolazu.**
*sah·moh sahm oo proh·lah·zoo*

I'd like to declare...
**Prijavio m/Prijavila f bih...**
*prih·yah·vih·oh/prih·yah·vih·lah bih...*

I have nothing to declare.
**Nemam ništa za prijaviti.**
*neh·mahm nih·shtah zah prih·yah·vih·tih*

## YOU MAY HEAR...

**Imate nešto za prijaviti?**
*ih·mah·teh neh·shtoh zah prih·yah·vih·tih*

Anything to declare?

**Za to morate platiti carinu.**
*zah toh moh·rah·teh plah·tih·tih tsah·rih·noo*

You must pay duty
on this.

**Otvorite tu torbu.**
*oh·tvoh·rih·teh too tohr·boo*

Open this bag.

## YOU MAY SEE...

| | |
|---|---|
| **CARINA** | customs |
| **ROBA OSLOBOĐENA CARINE** | duty-free goods |
| **ROBA ZA CARINJENJE** | goods to declare |
| **NIŠTA ZA CARINJENJE** | nothing to declare |
| **KONTROLA PUTOVNICA** | passport control |
| **POLICIJA** | police |

### ESSENTIAL

| | |
|---|---|
| Where's…? | **Gdje je…?** *gdyeh yeh…* |
| the ATM | **bankomat** *bahn·koh·maht* |
| the bank | **banka** *bahn·kah* |
| the currency exchange office | **mjenjačnica** *myeh·nyah·chnih·tsah* |
| What time does the bank open/close? | **Kada se banka otvara/zatvara?** *kah·dah seh bahh·kah oh·tvah·rah/zah·tvah·rah* |
| I'd like to change some dollars/pounds into kuna. | **Htio** *m*/**Htjela** *f* **bih promijeniti dolare/funte u kune.** *htih·oh/htyeh·lah bih proh·mih·yeh·nih·tih doh·lah·reh/foon·teh oo koo·neh* |
| I want to cash some traveler's checks [cheques]. | **Htio** *m*/**Htjela** *f* **bih unovčiti putničke čekove.** *htih·oh/htyeh·lah bih oo·noh·vchih·tih poot·nih·chkeh cheh·koh·veh* |

### At the Bank

| | |
|---|---|
| I'd like to… | **Htio** *m*/**Htjela** *f* **bih…** *htih·oh/htyeh·lah bih…* |
| change money | **promijeniti novac** *proh·mih·yeh·nih·tih noh·vahts* |
| change dollars/pounds into kuna | **promijeniti dolare/funte u kune** *proh·mih·yeh·nih·tih doh·lah·reh/foon·teh oo koo·neh* |
| cash travelers checks [cheques] | **unovčiti putničke čekove/euročekove** *oo·noh·vchih·tih poot·nih·chkeh cheh·koh·veh* |
| get a cash advance | **dobiti predujam** *doh·bih·tih preh·doo·yahm* |
| What's the exchange rate? | **Kakav je tečaj?** *kah·kahv yeh teh·chay* |
| How much commission do you charge? | **Kolika je provizija?** *koh·lih·kah yeh proh·vih·zih·yah* |

| I think there's a mistake. | **Mislim da je to greška.** *mih·slihm dah yeh toh greh·shkah.* |
| I've lost my traveler's checks [cheques]. | **Izgubio _m_/Izgubila _f_ sam putničke čekove.** *ihz·goo·bih·oh /ih·zgoo·bih·lah sahm poot·nih·chkeh cheh·koh·veh* |
| My card was... | **Moja kartica...** *moh·yah kahr·tih·tsah...* |
| lost | **je izgubljena** *yeh ihz·goo·blyeh·nah* |
| stolen. | **je ukradena** *yeh oo·krah·deh·nah* |
| doesn't work. | **ne radi** *neh rah·dih* |
| The ATM ate my card. | **Bankomat mi je progutao karticu.** *bahh·koh·maht mih yeh proh·goo·tah·oh kahr·tih·tsoo* |

For Numbers, see page 169.

At some banks, cash can be obtained from ATMs with Visa™, Eurocard™, American Express® and many other international cards. Instructions are often given in English. Banks with a Change sign will exchange foreign currency. You can also change money at travel agencies and hotels, but the rate will not be as good. Remember to bring your passport when you want to change money.

## YOU MAY SEE...

| | |
|---|---|
| **OVDJE UBACITE KARTICU** | insert card |
| **PONIŠTI** | cancel |
| **BRIŠI** | clear |
| **UNOS** | enter |
| **PIN** | PIN |
| **PODIZANJE NOVCA** | withdrawal |
| **SA TEKUĆEG RAČUNA** | from checking [current] account |
| **SA ŠTEDNOG RAČUNA** | from savings account |
| **RAČUN** | receipt |

## YOU MAY SEE...

The Croatian currency is the **kuna**, divided into **lipa**.
**1 kuna = 100 lipa**
Coins: 1, 2, 5, 10, 50 **lipa** and 1, 2, 5, 25 **kuna**
Bills: 5, 10, 20, 50, 100, 200, 500, 1000 **kuna**
**The euro is also widely accepted.**

# Getting Around

## ESSENTIAL

| | |
|---|---|
| How do I get to town? | **Kako mogu stići do grada?** *kah·koh moh·goo stih·chih doh grah·dah* |
| Where's...? | **Gdje je...?** *gdyeh yeh...* |
| the airport | **zračna luka** *zrah·chnah loo·kah* |
| the train [railway] station | **željeznički kolodvor** *zheh·lyeh·znih·chkih koh·loh·dvohr* |
| the bus station | **autobusni kolodvor** *ah·oo·toh·boo·snih koh·loh·dvohr* |
| How far is it? | **Koliko je daleko?** *koh·lih·koh yeh dah·leh·koh* |
| Where do I buy a ticket? | **Gdje kupujem kartu?** *gdyeh koo·poo·yehm kahr·too* |
| A one-way/ return-trip ticket to... | **Jednu kartu u jednom smjeru/povratnu do...** *yeh·dnoo kahr·too oo yeh·dnohm smyeh·roo/ poh·vrah·tnoo doh...* |
| How much? | **Koliko?** *koh·lih·koh* |
| Is there a discount? | **Ima li popust?** *ih·mah lih poh·poost* |
| Which gate? | **Koji izlaz?** *koh·yih ihz·lahz* |
| Which line? | **Koja linija?** *koh·yah lee·nih·ya* |
| Which platform? | **Koji peron?** *koh·yih peh·rohn* |
| Where can I get a taxi? | **Gdje mogu uzeti taksi?** *gdyeh moh·goo oo·zeh·tih tah·ksee* |
| Take me to this address. | **Odvedite me do ove adrese.** *ohd·veh·dih·teh meh doh oh·veh ah·dreh·seh* |
| Where's the car rental [hire]? | **Gdje je rent-a-car?** *gdyeh yeh rehn·tah·kahr* |
| Can I have a map? | **Mogu li dobiti kartu?** *moh·goo lih doh·bih·tih kahr·too* |

# Tickets

| | |
|---|---|
| When's...to Zagreb? | **Kada ima...za Zagreb?** |
| | *kah·dah ih·mah...zah zah·grehb* |
| (first) bus | **(prvi) autobus** *(pr·vee)* ah·oo·toh·boos |
| | **(next) flight** *(sljedeći) let (slyeh·deh·chih) leht* |
| | **(last) train** *(posljednji) vlak (poh·slyeh·dnyih) vlahk* |
| Is there...trip? | **Ima li...put?** *ih·mah lih...poot* |
| an earlier | **raniji** *rah·nih·yee* |
| a later | **kasniji** *kah·snih·yee* |
| an overnight | **noćni** *noh·chnih* |
| a cheaper | **jeftiniji** *yeh·ftih·nih·yee* |
| Where do I buy | **Gdje mogu kupiti kartu?** |
| a ticket? | *gdyeh moh·goo koo·pih·tih kahr·too* |
| One/two ticket(s), | **Jednu kartu/Dvije karte, molim Vas.** |
| please. | *yeh·dnoo kahr·too/dvih·yeh kahr·teh moh·lihm vahs* |
| For today/tomorrow. | **Za danas/sutra.** *zah dah·nahs/soo·trah* |
| A...ticket. | **Jednu kartu...** *yeh·dnoo kahr·too...* |
| one-way | **u jednom smjeru** *oo yeh·dnohm smyeh·roo* |
| round-trip [return] | **povratnu** *poh·vrah·tnoo* |
| first class | **za prvu klasu** *zah prvoo klah·soo* |
| business class | **za biznis klasu** *zah bihz·nihs klah·soo* |
| economy class | **za ekonomsku klasu** *zah eh·koh·nohm·skoo klah·soo* |
| one-day | **za jedan dan** *zah yeh·dahn dahn* |
| multiple-trip | **za višekratno putovanje** |
| | *zah vih·sheh·krah·tnoh poo·toh·vah·nyeh* |
| The express bus/ | **Brzi autobus/vlak, molim Vas.** |
| train, please. | *br·zih ah·oo·toh·boos/vlahk moh·lihm vahs* |
| The local bus/train, | **Lokalni autobus/vlak, molim** |
| please. | *loh·kahl·nih ah·oo·toh·boo·s/vlah·kh, moh·lih·m* |
| How much? | **Koliko?** *koh·lih·koh* |
| Is there...discount? | **Ima li popust za...?** *ih·mah lih poh·poost zah...* |

| a child | **djecu** *dyeh·tsoo* |
| a student | **studente** *stoo·dehh·teh* |
| a senior citizen | **umirovljenike** *oo·mih·roh·vlyeh·nee·keh* |
| a tourist | **turiste** *too·rih·steh* |
| I have an e-ticket. | **Imam e-kartu.** *ih·mahm ee·kahr·too* |
| Can I buy a ticket on the bus/train? | **Mogu li kupiti kartu u autobusu/vlaku?** *moh·goo lih koo·pih·tih kahr·too oo ah·oo·toh·boo·soo/vlah·koo* |
| Do I have to stamp the ticket before boarding? | **Moram li ovjeriti kartu prije ukrcavanja?** *moh·rahm lih oh·vyeh·rih·tih kahr·too prih·yeh oo·kr·tsah·vah·nyah* |
| How long is this ticket valid? | **Koliko važi ova karta?** *koh·lih·koh vah·zhih oh·vah kahr·tah* |
| Can I return on the same ticket? | **Mogu li se vratiti s istom kartom?** *moh·goo lih seh vrah·tih·tih sih·stohm kahr·tohm* |
| I'd like to... my reservation. | **Htio** *m*/**Htjela** *f* **bih... svoju rezervaciju.** *htih·oh/htyeh·lah bih... svoh·yoo reh·zehr·vah·tsih·yoo* |
| cancel | **poništiti** *poh·nih·shtih·tih* |
| change | **promijeniti** *proh·mee·yeh·nih·tih* |
| confirm | **potvrditi** *poh·tvr·dih·tih* |

For Days, see page 171.

## Plane

### Airport Transfer

| How much is a taxi to the airport? | **Koliko košta taksi do zračne luke?** *koh·lih·koh koh·shtah tah·ksee doh zrah·chneh loo·keh* |
| To...Airport, please. | **Do zračne luke..., molim Vas.** *doh zrah·chneh loo·keh...moh·lihm vahs* |
| My airline is... | **Moja zrakoplovna kompanija je...** *moh·yah zrah·koh·ploh·vnah kohm·pah·nih·yah yeh...* |
| My flight leaves at... | **Moj let je u...** *mohy leht yeh oo...* |
| I'm in a rush. | **Žurim.** *zhoo·rihm* |

## YOU MAY SEE...

| | |
|---|---|
| **DOLASCI** | arrivals |
| **POLASCI** | departures |
| **PREUZIMANJE PRTLJAGE** | baggage claim |
| **SIGURNOSNA KONTROLA** | security |
| **DOMAĆI LETOVI** | domestic flights |
| **MEĐUNARODNI LETOVI** | international flights |
| **REGISTRIRANJE PUTNIKA** | check-in desk |
| **REGISTRIRANJE ZA E-KARTE** | e-ticket check-in |
| **IZLAZI ZA ODLASKE** | departure gates |

## YOU MAY HEAR...

**S kojom kompanijom letite?**
*skoh·yohm kohm·pah·nih·yohm leh·tih·teh*
**Domaćom ili međunarodnom?**
*doh·mah·chohm ih·lih meh·joo·nah·roh·dnohm*
**Koji izlaz?** *koh·yih ihz·lahz*

What airline
are you flying?
Domestic or
International?
What terminal?

Can you take an
alternate route?
**Možete li voziti drugim putem?**
*moh·zheh·teh lih voh·zih·tih droo·gihm poo·tehm*

Can you drive faster/
slower ?
**Možete li voziti brže/sporije?**
*moh·zheh·teh lih voh·zih·tih br·zheh/spoh·rih·yeh*

For Time, see page 170.

## Checking In

Where is check-in? **Gdje je registriranje?** *gdyeh jeh reh·gih·strih·rah·nyeh*
My name is... **Moje ime je...** *moh·yeh ih·meh yeh...*

| I'm going to… | **Idem u…** *ih·dehm oo…* |
| Here's my reservation | **Evo moje rezervacije** *eh·voh moh·yeh reh·zheh·rvah·tsee·yeh* |
| I have… | **Imam…** *ih·mahm…* |
| one suitcase | **jedan kofer** *yeh·dahn koh·fehr* |
| two suitcases | **dva kofera** *dvah koh·feh·rah* |
| one carry-on [piece of hand luggage] | **jedan komad ručne prtljage** *yeh·dahn koh·mahd roo·chneh prt·lyah·geh* |
| How much luggage is allowed? | **Koliko je dozvoljeno prtljage?** *koh·lih·koh yeh doh·zvoh·lyeh·noh prt·lyah·geh* |
| Is that pounds or kilos? | **Jesu li to funte ili kilogrami?** *yeh·soo lih toh foon·teh ih·lih kih·loh·grah·mih* |
| Which terminal/gate? | **Koji terminal/izlaz?** *koh·yih tehr·mih·nahl/ihz·lahz* |
| I'd like a window/ an aisle seat. | **Htio** *m***/Htjela** *f* **bih sjedalo do prozora/prolaza.** *htih·oh/htye·lah bih syeh·dah·loh doh proh·zoh·rah/proh·lah·zah* |
| When do we leave/arrive? | **Kada krećemo/stižemo?** *kah·dah kreh·cheh·moh/stih·zheh·moh* |
| Is the flight delayed? | **Kasni li let?** *kah·snih lih leht* |
| How late? | **Koliko kasni?** *koh·lih·koh kah·snih* |

## YOU MAY HEAR...

**Sljedeći!** *slyeh·deh·chih* — Next!

**Vašu putovnicu/kartu, molim Vas.** *vah·shoo poo·toh·vnih·tsoo/kahr·too moh·lihm vahs* — Your passport/ticket, please.

**Imate li prtljage?** *ih·mah·teh lih prt·lyah·geh* — Are you checking any luggage?

**Imate višak prtljage.** *ih·mah·teh vih·shahk prt·lyah·geh* — You have excess luggage.

**To je preveliko za ručnu prtljagu.** *toh yeh preh·veh·lih·koh zah roo·chnoo prt·lyah·goo* — That's too large for a carry-on [to carry on board].

**Jeste li sami pakirali svoje kofere?** *yeh·steh lih sah·mih pah·kee·rah·lih svoh·yeh koh·feh·reh* — Did you pack these bags yourself?

**Je li Vam itko dao bilo što da ponesete?** *yeh lih vahm ih·tkoh dah·oh bih·loh shtoh dah poh·neh·seh·teh* — Did anyone give you anything to carry?

**Izujte cipele** *ih·zooy·teh cih·peh·leh* — Take off your shoes.

**Ukrcavanje...** *oo·kr·tsah·vah·nyeh...* — Now boarding flight...

## Luggage

| Where is/are...? | **Gdje je/su...?** *gdyeh yeh/soo...* |
|---|---|
| the luggage carts [trolleys] | **kolica za prtljagu** *prtljagu koh·lee·tsah zah prt·lyah·goo* |
| the luggage lockers | **pretinci za prtljagu** *preh·tihn·tsih zah prt·lyah·goos* |

| the baggage claim | **preuzimanje prtljage** |
| | *preh·oo·zih·mah·nyeh prt·lyah·geh* |
| My luggage has been lost/stolen. | **Moja prtljaga je izgubljena/ukradena** |
| | *moh·yah prt·lyah·gah yeh ihz·goo·blyeh·nah/ oo·krah·deh·nah* |
| My suitcase was damaged. | **Moj kofer je oštećen.** |
| | *mohy koh·fehr yeh oh·shteh·chehn* |

## Finding your Way

| Where is…? | **Gdje je/su…?** *gdyeh yeh/soo…* |
| the currency exchange office | **mjenjačnica** *myeh·nyah·chnih·tsah* |
| the car hire | **rent-a-car** *rehnt·ah·kahr* |
| the exit | **izlaz** *ihz·lahz* |
| the taxi stand [rank] | **taksiji** *tah·ksih·yih* |
| Is there…into town? | **Ima li…do grada?** *ih·mah lih…doh grah·dah* |
| a bus | **autobus** *ah·oo·toh·boos* |
| a train | **vlak** *vlahk* |
| a tram | **tramvaj** *trahm·vahy* |

For Asking Directions, see page 34.

## Train

| Where's the train [railway] station? | **Gdje je željeznički kolodvor?** |
| | *gdyeh yeh zheh·lyeh·znih·chkih koh·loh·dvohr* |
| How far is it? | **Koliko je daleko?** *koh·lih·koh yeh dah·leh·koh* |
| Where is/are…? | **Gdje je/su…?** *gdyeh yeh/soo…* |
| the ticket office | **prodaja karata** *proh·dah·yah kah·rah·tah* |
| the information desk | **informacije** *ihn·fohr·mah·tsih·yeh* |
| the luggage lockers | **pretinci za prtljagu** *preh·tihn·tsih zah prt·lyah·goo* |

| | |
|---|---|
| the platforms | **peroni** *peh·roh·nih* |
| Can I have a schedule [timetable]? | **Mogu li dobiti raspored vožnje?** *moh·goo lih doh·bih·tih rah·spoh·rehd voh·zhnyeh* |
| How long is the trip? | **Koliko traje put?** *koh·lih·koh trah·yeh poot* |
| Is it a direct train? | **Ima li direktni vlak?** *ih·mah lih dih·reh·ktnih vlahk* |
| Do I have to change trains? | **Moram li presjedati?** *moh·rahm lih preh·syeh·dah·tih* |
| Is the train on time? | **Stiže li vlak na vrijeme?** *stih·zheh lih vlahk nah vrih·yeh·meh* |

For Tickets, see page 19.

---

## YOU MAY SEE…

| | |
|---|---|
| **PERONI** | platforms |
| **INFORMACIJE** | information |
| **REZERVACIJE** | reservations |
| **ČEKAONICA** | waiting room |
| **DOLASCI** | arrivals |
| **POLASCI** | departures |

Croatia's main train network is **HŽ**, **Hrvatske željeznice**. **HŽ** offers a variety of train types, from express to local, national and international. You can purchase tickets or make reservations through travel agencies or at the station.

## Departures

| Which track [platform] to…? | **Koji je peron za…?** |
| | koh·yih yeh peh·rohn zah… |
| Is this the platform/ train to…? | **Je li ovo peron/vlak za…?** |
| | yeh lih oh·voh peh·rohn/vlahk zah… |
| Where is platform…? | **Gdje je peron…?** gdyeh yeh peh·rohn… |
| Where do I change for…? | **Gdje presjedam za…?** |
| | gdyeh preh·syeh·dahm zah… |

## On Board

| Can I sit here/open the window? | **Mogu li sjesti ovdje/otvoriti prozor?** |
| | moh·goo lih syeh·stih ohv·dyeh/oh·tvoh·rih·tih proh·zohr |

## YOU MAY HEAR…

**Ukrcavanje!** oo·kr·tsah·vah·nyeh — All aboard!
**Karte, molim Vas** kahr·teh moh·lihm vahs — Tickets, please.
**Kamo?** kah·moh — Where to?
**Koliko karata?** koh·lih·koh kah·rah·tah — How many tickets?
**Trebate presjesti u…** — You have to change at…
treh·bah·teh preh·syeh·stih oo…
**Sljedeća stanica…** — Next stop…
slyeh·deh·chah stah·nih·tsah…

| That's my seat. | **To je moje mjesto.** *toh yeh moh·yeh myeh·stoh* |
| Here's my reservation. | **To je moja rezervacija.** *toh yeh moh·yah reh·zehr·vah·tsih·yah* |

## Bus

| Where's the bus station? | **Gdje je autobusni kolodvor?** *gdyeh yeh ah·oo·toh·boo·snih koh·loh·dvohr* |
| How far is it? | **Koliko je daleko?** *koh·lih·koh yeh dah·leh·koh* |
| How do I get to…? | **Kako mogu stići do…?** *kah·koh moh·goo stih·chih doh…* |
| Is this the bus to…? | **Je li ovo autobus za…?** *yeh lih oh·voh ah·oo·toh·boos zah…* |
| Can you tell me when to get off? | **Možete li mi reći kada trebam sići?** *moh·zheh·teh lih mih reh·chih kah·dah treh·bahm sih·chih* |
| Do I have to change buses? | **Moram li presjedati?** *moh·rahm lih preh·syeh·dah·tih* |
| How many stops to…? | **Koliko ima stanica do…?** *koh·lih·koh ih·mah stah·nih·tsah doh…* |
| Stop here, please! | **Stanite ovdje, molim Vas!** *stah·nih·teh ohv·dyeh moh·lihm vahs* |

The bus service is extensive in Croatia. Bus stations are generally well organized with clearly listed **dolasci** (arrivals) and **polasci** or **odlasci** (departures). Regular international bus lines connect Croatia with all neighboring countries and most countries throughout Europe. Tickets should be bought before boarding at bus stations. When boarding long distance buses, give the ticket to the driver; when boarding local buses, stamp your ticket using the validation machine, located on the bus.

**YOU MAY SEE...**

| | |
|---|---|
| **AUTOBUSNA POSTAJA** | bus stop |
| **ULAZ/IZLAZ** | enter/exit |
| **ZATRAŽI ZAUSTAVLJANJE** | request stop |
| **PONIŠTI KARTU** | stamp your ticket |

## Tram

Where's the tram stop? **Gdje je tramvajska stanica?**
*gdyeh yeh trahm·vahy·skah stah·nih·tsah*

A map, please. **Molim Vas kartu/mapu.**
*moh·lihm vahs kahr·too/mah·poo*

Which line for...? **Koja linija vozi za...?** *koh·ya lee·nih·yah voh·zih zah*

Which direction? **U kojem smjeru?** *oo koh·yehm smyeh·roo*

Do I have to transfer **Moram li presjedati?**
[change]? *moh·rahm lih preh·sjeh·da·tih*

Is this the tram to...? **Je li ovo tramvaj za...?** *yeh·lih oh·voh trahm·vahyzah*

How many stops **Koliko ima stanica do...?**
to...? *koh·lih·koh ih·mah stah·nih·tsah doh...*

Where are we? **Gdje smo sada?** *gdyeh smoh sah·dah*

For Tickets, see page 19.

In Zagreb, trams and buses are available; elsewhere, buses are the main method of public transportation, see page 27. For local service within a town, tickets can be purchased from newsstands and tobacconists; they can also be purchased as you board the bus. In Zagreb you can purchase a Zagreb card at the tourist information office. The card is valid for 72 hours on all public transportation, and includes a discounted rate for entry into local museums.

## Boat & Ferry

| | |
|---|---|
| When is the ferry to…? | **Kada ide trajekt za…?**<br>*kah·dah ih·deh trah·yehkt zah…* |
| Can I take my car? | **Mogu li povesti i svoj auto?** *moh·goo lih poh·veh·stih*<br>*ih svohy ah·oo·toh?* |
| What time is the next sailing? | **Kada je sljedeće isplovljavanje?**<br>*kah·dah yeh slyeh·deh·cheh ih·splohv·lyahv·ah·nyeh* |
| Can I book a seat/cabin? | **Mogu li rezervirati sjedalo/kabinu?**<br>*moh·goo lih reh·zehr·vih·rah·tih syeh·dah·loh/*<br>*kah·beenuh* |
| How long is the crossing? | **Koliko dugo traje prijelaz?**<br>*koh·lih·koh doo·goh trah·yeh prih·yeh·lahz* |
| Where are the life jackets? | **Gdje su prsluci za spašavanje?**<br>*gdyeh soo prs·loo·tsih zah spah·shah·vah·nyeh* |

---

### YOU MAY SEE…

| | |
|---|---|
| **ČAMAC ZA SPAŠAVANJE** | life boats |
| **ZABRANJEN PRISTUP** | no access |
| **PRSLUCI ZA SPAŠAVANJE** | life jackets |

Ferry services link the Croatian mainland with Adriatic islands. **Jadrolinija** (www.jadrolinija.hr) is the main state owned ferry corporation which maintains the largest number of international and domestic ferry and shipping lines. Its main office is in Rijeka.

## Taxi

| | |
|---|---|
| Where can I get a taxi? | **Gdje mogu uzeti taksi?** |
| | *gdyeh moh·goo oo·zeh·tih tah·ksee* |
| Can you send a taxi? | **Možete li poslati taksi?** |
| | *moh·zheh·teh lih poh·slah·tih tah·ksih* |
| Do you have the number for a taxi? | **Imate li broj taksija?** |
| | *ih·mah·teh lih brohy tah·ksih·yah* |
| I'/I'd like a taxi now/ in an hour. | **Htio *m*/Htjela *f* bih taksi sada/za sat vremena.** |
| | *htih·oh/htyeh·lah bih tah·ksee sah·dah/zah saht vreh·meh·nah* |
| Pick me up at... | **Dođite po mene u...** *doh·jih·teh poh meh·neh oo...* |
| I'm going to... | **Idem do...** *ih·dehm doh...* |
| this address | **ove adrese** *oh·veh ah·dreh·seh* |
| the airport | **zračne luke** *zrah·chneh loo·keh* |

Taxis are generally expensive in Croatia. Extra fees are usually charged for trips to the airport, to bus and train stations and for extra luggage. When entering the taxi, make sure the meter is turned on; it should register a base fare when the trip begins. The fare is then increased by a set amount per kilometer traveled. A 10% tip to the driver is customary.

## YOU MAY HEAR...

**Kamo?** *kah·moh* — Where to?

**Koja je adresa?** *koh·yah yeh ah·dreh·sah* — What's the address?

**Ima tarifa noćna/za zračnu luku.**
*ih·mah lih tah·rih·fah noh·chnah/zah zrah·chnoo loo·koo* — There's a nighttime/airport surcharge.

| | |
|---|---|
| the train [railway] station | **željezničkog kolodvora** *zheh·lyeh·znih·chkohg koh·loh·dvoh·rah* |
| I'm late. | **Kasnim.** *kah·snihm* |
| Can you drive faster/slower? | **Možete li voziti brže/sporije?** *moh·zheh·teh lih voh·zih·tih brzheh/spoh·rih·yeh* |
| Stop/Wait here. | **Stanite/Čekajte ovdje.** *stah·nih·teh/cheh·kahy·teh ohv·dyeh* |
| How much? | **Koliko?** *koh·lih·koh* |
| You said it would cost... | **Rekli ste da je koštati...** *reh·klih steh dah cheh koh·shtah·tih...* |
| Keep the change. | **Zadržite ostatak.** *zah·drzhih·teh oh·stah·tahk* |

## Bicycle & Motorbike

| | |
|---|---|
| I'd like to rent [hire]... | **Htio** *m***/Htjela** *f* **bih iznajmiti...** *htih·oh /htyeh·lah bih ihz·nahy·mih·tih...* |
| a bicycle | **bicikl** *bih·tsihkl* |
| a moped | **moped** *moh·pehd* |
| a motorcycle | **motor** *moh·tohr* |
| How much per day/week? | **Koliko košta po danu/tjednu?** *koh·lih·koh koh·shta poh dah·noo/tyeh·dnoo* |
| Can I have a helmet/lock? | **Mogu li dobiti kacigu/lanac?** *moh·goo lih doh·bih·tih kah·tsih·goo/lah·nahts* |

| I have a puncture/<br>flat tyre | **Guma mi je probušena/prazna**<br>*goo·mah mih yeh proh·bu·sheh·nah/prah·znah* |

## Car Hire

| Where's the car<br>rental [hire]? | **Gdje je rent-a-car?** *gdyeh yeh rehn·tah·kahr* |
| I'd like… | **Htio** *m*/**Htjela** *f* **bih** *htih·oh/htyeh·lah bih…* |
| a cheap/small car | **jeftini/mali automobil**<br>*yeh·ftih·nih/mah·lih ah·oo·toh·moh·bihl* |
| an automatic/<br>a manual | **automatik/automobil s ručnim mjenjačem**<br>*ah·oo·toh·mah·tihk/ah·oo·toh·moh·bihl s roo·chnihm*<br>*myeh·nyah·chehm* |
| a 2-/4-door | **s dvoja/četvora vrata** *s dvoh·yah/cheht·voh·rah vrah·tah* |
| air conditioning | **klima-uređaj** *klih·mah oo·reh·jahy* |
| a car seat | **sjedalo za djete** *syeh·dah·loh zah dyeh·teh* |
| How much…? | **Koliko je…?** *koh·lih·koh yeh…* |
| per day/week | **po danu/tjednu** *poh dah·noo/tyeh·dnoo* |
| for…days | **za…dana** *zah…dah·nah* |
| per kilometer | **po kilometru** *poh kih·loh·meh·troo* |
| for unlimited<br>mileage | **za neograničenu kilometražu**<br>*zah neh·oh·grah·nih·cheh·noo kih·loh·meh·trah·zhoo* |
| with insurance | **sa osiguranjem** *sah oh·sih·goo·rah·nyehm* |

| Are there any discounts? | **Ima li popust?** *ih·mah lih poh·poost* |
| Where's the parking meter? | **(Gdje je) automat za parkiranje?** *gdyeh yeh ah·oo·toh·mah·t zah pahr·kih·rah·nyeh* |
| Where's... the parking garage? | **(Gdje je...) garaža?** *gdyeh yeh ... gah·rah·zhah* |

## YOU MAY HEAR...

**Imate li međunarodnu vozačku dozvolu?**
*ih·mah·teh lih meh·joo·nah·roh·dnoo voh·zah·chkoo doh·zvoh·loo*

Do you have an international driver's license?

**Vašu putovnicu, molim**
*Vas. vah·shoo poo·toh·vnih·tsoo moh·lihm vahs*

Your passport, please.

**Želite li osiguranje?**
*zheh·lih·teh lih oh·sih·goo·rah·nyeh*

Do you want insurance?

**Trebate platiti kauciju.**
*treh·bah·teh plah·tih·tih kah·oo·tsih·yoo*

I'll need a deposit.

**Upišite inicijale/Potpišite ovdje.** *oo·pih·shih·teh ih·nih·tsih·yah·leh/poht·pih·shih·teh ohv·dyeh*

Initial/Sign here.

## Fuel Station

| Where's the gas [petrol] station? | **Gdje je benzinska postaja?** *gdyeh yeh behn·zihn·skah poh·stah·yah* |
| Fill it up. | **Napunite do vrha.** *nah·poo·nih·teh doh vrhah* |
| ...kuna, please. | **...kuna, molim Vas.** *... koo·nah moh·lihm vahs* |
| I'll pay in cash/ by credit card. | **Plaćam gotovinom/kreditnom karticom.** *plah·chahm goh·toh·vih·nohm/kreh·diht·nohm kahr·tih·tsohm* |

## YOU MAY SEE...

| | |
|---|---|
| **GORIVO** | gas [petrol] |
| **BEZOLOVNI** | unleaded |
| **OBIČNI** | regular |
| **SUPER** | super |
| **DIZEL** | diesel |
| **SAMOPOSLUŽIVANJE** | self-service |
| **POTPUNA USLUGA** | full-service |

## Asking Directions

| | |
|---|---|
| Is this the way to...? | **Je li ovo put za...?** *yeh lih oh·voh poot zah...* |
| How far is it to...? | **Koliko je daleko do...?** *koh·lih·koh yeh dah·leh·koh doh...* |
| Where's...? | **Gdje je...?** *gdyeh yeh...* |
| ...Street | **Ulica...** *oo·lih·tsah...* |
| this address | **ova adresa** *oh·vah ah·dreh·sah* |
| the highway [motorway] | **autoput** *ah·oo·toh·poot* |
| Can you show me on the map? | **Možete li mi pokazati na karti?** *moh·zheh·teh lih mih poh·kah·zah·tih nah kahr·tih* |
| I'm lost. | **Izgubio m/Izgubila f sam se.** *ihz·goo·bih·oh/ihz·goo·bih·lah sahm seh* |

## Parking

| | |
|---|---|
| Can I park here? | **Mogu li ovdje parkirati?** *moh·goo lih ohv·dyeh pahr·kih·rah·tih* |
| Where's the...? | **Gdje je...?** *gdyeh yeh...* |
| parking garage | **parking garaža** *pahr·kihng gah·rah·zhah* |
| parking lot [car park] | **parkiralište** *pahr·kih·rah·lih·shteh* |

| parking meter | **automat na parkiralištu** |
| | *ah·oo·toh·maht nah pahr·kihr·rah·lih·shtoo* |
| How much…? | **Koliko…?** *koh·lih·koh…* |
| per hour | **po satu** *poh sah·too* |

---

### YOU MAY HEAR…

| | |
| --- | --- |
| **pravo** *prah·voh* | straight ahead |
| **lijevo** *lih·yeh·voh* | left |
| **desno** *deh·snoh* | right |
| **na uglu** *nah oo·gloo* | on the corner |
| **iza ugla** *ih·zah oo·glah* | around the corner |
| **prekoputa** *preh·koh·poo·tah* | opposite |
| **iza** *ih·zah* | behind |
| **pored** *poh·rehd* | next to |
| **poslije** *poh·slih·yeh* | after |
| **sjever/jug** *syeh·vehr/yoog* | north/south |
| **istok/zapad** *ih·stohk/zah·pahd* | east/west |
| **na semaforu** *nah seh·mah·foh·roo* | at the traffic light |
| **na raskrižju** *nah rah·skrih·zhyoo* | at the intersection |

| per day | **po danu** *poh dah-noo* |
| overnight | **preko noći** *preh-koh noh-chih* |

Public parking is marked with a **P** sign. Tickets can be bought at nearby parking machines. There are heavy fines for cars left in no parking zones, and cars parked dangerously will be towed away. Wheel clamps are also in operation.

## YOU MAY SEE...

 **STOP** — stop

 **PUT BEZ PRVENSTVA PROLAZA** — yield

 **ZABRANJENO PARKIRANJE** — no parking

 **JEDNOSMJERNA ULICA** — one way

 **OPASNA OKUKA** — dangerous bend

 **OGRANIČENJE BRZINE** — maximum speed limit

 **ZABRANETO ZASTANUVANJE** — no stopping

 **ZABRANETO PRETEKNUVANJE** — no passing

 **ZABRANJEN PROLAZ** — no entry

## Breakdown & Repair

| | |
|---|---|
| My car broke down/ won't start. | **Moj automobil se pokvario/ne kreće.** *mohy ah·oo·toh·moh·bihl seh poh·kvah·rih·oh/neh kreh·cheh* |
| Can you fix it (today)? | **Možete li ga popraviti (danas)?** *moh·zheh·teh lih gah poh·prah·vih·tih (dah·nahs)* |
| When will it be ready? | **Kada će biti gotov?** *kah·dah cheh bih·tih goh·tohv* |
| How much? | **Koliko?** *koh·lih·koh* |
| I have a puncture/ flat tyre. | **Guma mi je probušena/prazna.** *goo·mah mih yeh proh·bu·sheh·nah/prah·znah* |

## Accidents

| | |
|---|---|
| There was an accident. | **Dogodila se nezgoda.** *doh·goh·dih·lah seh neh·zgoh·dah* |
| Call… | **Pozovite…** *poh·zoh·vih·teh…* |
| an ambulance | **hitnu pomoć** *hih·tnoo poh·mohch* |
| the fire department | **vatrogasce** *vah·troh·gah·stseh* |
| the police | **policiju** *poh·lih·tsih·yoo* |

## Places to Stay

### ESSENTIAL

| | |
|---|---|
| Can you recommend a hotel? | **Možete li mi preporučiti hotel?** *moh·zheh·teh lih mih preh·poh·roo·chih·tih hoh·tehl* |
| I have a reservation. | **Imam rezervaciju.** *ih·mahm reh·zehr·vah·tsih·yoo* |
| My name is… | **Moje ime je…** *moh·yeh ih·meh yeh…* |
| Do you have a room…? | **Imate li sobu…?** *ih·mah·teh lih soh·boo…* |
| for one/two | **za jednu osobu/dvije osobe** *zah yeh·dnoo oh·soh·buh/dvih·yeh oh·soh·beh* |
| with a bathroom | **s kupaonicom** *s koo·pah·oh·nih·tsohm* |
| with air conditioning | **s klima-uređajem** *s klih·mah oo·reh·jah·yehm* |
| For… | **Za…** *zah…* |
| tonight | **večeras** *veh·cheh·rahs* |
| two nights | **dvije noći** *dvih·yeh noh·chih* |
| one week | **tjedan dana** *tyeh·dahn dah·nah* |
| How much? | **Koliko?** *koh·lih·koh* |
| Is there anything cheaper? | **Ima li nešto jeftinije?** *ih·mah lih neh·shtoh jeh·ftih·nih·yeh* |
| When's check-out? | **Kada moramo napustiti?** *kah·dah moh·rah·moh nah·poo·stih·tih* |
| Can I leave this in the safe? | **Mogu li ostaviti ovo u sefu?** *moh·goo lih oh·stah·vih·tih oh·voh oo seh·foo* |
| Can I leave my bags? | **Mogu li ostaviti torbe?** *moh·goo lih oh·stah·vih·tih tohr·beh* |
| Can I have my bill/ a receipt? | **Mogu li dobiti račun/priznanicu?** *moh·goo lih doh·bih·tih rah·choon/prih·znah·nih·tsoo* |
| I'll pay in cash/by credit card. | **Plaćam gotovinom/kreditnom karticom.** *plah·chahm goh·toh·vih·nohm/kreh·dih·tnohm kahr·tih·tsohm* |

Visit the local **Hrvatska turistička zajednica**, **HTZ** (Croatian National Tourist Board), for recommendations on places to stay. The staff can usually supply accommodation details and maps of towns. Hours vary according to how busy they are.

## Somewhere to Stay

| | |
|---|---|
| Can you recommend…? | **Možete li preporučiti…?** *moh·zheh·teh lih preh·poh·roo·chih·tih…* |
| a hotel | **hotel** *hoh·tehl* |
| a hostel | **hostel** *hoh·stehl* |
| a campsite | **kamp** *kahmp* |
| a bed and breakfast | **polupansion** *poh·loo·pahn·sih·ohn* |
| What is it near? | **Što se nalazi u blizini?** *shtoh seh nah·lah·zih oo blih·zih·nih* |
| How do I get there? | **Kako mogu stići tamo?** *kah·koh moh·goo stih·chih tah·moh* |

## At the Hotel

| | |
|---|---|
| I have a reservation. | **Imam rezervaciju.** *ih·mahm reh·zehr·vah·tsih·yoo* |
| My name is… | **Moje ime je…** *moh·yeh ih·meh yeh…* |
| Do you have a room…? | **Imate li sobu…?** *ih·mah·teh lih soh·boo…* |
| for one | **za jednu osobu** *zah yeh·dnoo oh·soh·boo* |
| for two | **za dvije osobe** *zah dvih·yeh oh·soh·beh* |
| with a bathroom [toilet]/shower | **s kupaonicom/tušem** *s koo·pah·oh·nih·tsohm/too·shehm* |
| with air conditioning | **s klima-uređajem** *s klih·mah oo·reh·jah·yehm* |
| Do you have a room…? | **Imate li sobu…?** *ih·mah·teh lih soh·boo…* |

### YOU MAY HEAR...

**Vašu putovnicu/kreditnu karticu, molim**
*Vas. vah·shoo poo·toh·vnih·tsoo/kreh·dih·tnoo
kahr·tih·tsoo moh·lihm vahs*

Your passport/credit card, please.

**Popunite ovaj obrazac.**
*poh·poo·nih·teh oh·vahy oh·brah·zahts*

Fill out this form.

**Potpišite ovdje.** *poht·pih·shih·teh ohv·dyeh*

Sign here.

| | |
|---|---|
| with a single/ double bed | **s jednim/bračnim krevetom** *s yeh·dnihm/brah·chnihm kreh·veh·tohm* |
| that's handicapped [disabled] accessible | **s pristupom za hendikepirane osobe** *s prih·stoo·pohm zah hehn·dih·keh·pih·rah·neh oh·soh·beh* |
| on the ground floor | **na prizemlju** *nah prih·zeh·mlyoo* |
| that's smoking/ non-smoking | **predviđene za pušače/nepušače** *preh·dvih·jeh·neh zah poo·shah·cheh/neh·poo·shah·cheh* |
| For... | **Za...** *zah...* |
| tonight | **večeras** *veh·cheh·rahs* |
| two nights | **dvije noći** *dvih·yeh noh·chih* |
| a week | **tjedan dana** *tyeh·dahn dah·nah* |
| Where can I park? | **Gdje mogu parkirati?** *gdyeh moh·goo pahr·kih·rah·tih* |
| Do you have...? | **Imate li...?** *ih·mah·teh lih...* |
| a computer | **računar** *rah·choo·nahr* |
| an elevator [a lift] | **lift** *lihft* |
| (wireless) internet service | **(bežični) internet** *(beh·zhih·chnih) ihn·tehr·neht* |
| room service | **poslugu** *poh·sloo·goo* |
| a TV | **televizor** *teh·leh·vih·zohr* |
| a pool | **bazen** *bah·zehn* |
| a gym | **teretanu** *tah·reh·tah·noo* |

| I need... | **Treba mi...** treh·bah mih... |
| an extra bed | **dodatni krevet** doh·dah·tnih kreh·veht |
| a cot | **kolijevka** koh·lih·yehv·kah |
| a crib | **dječiji krevetić** dyeh·chih·yih kreh·veh·tihch |

## Price

| How much per night/week? | **Koliko košta za noć/tjedan?** koh·lih·koh koh·shtah zah nohch/tyeh·dahn |
| Does that include breakfast/sales tax [VAT]? | **Je li doručak/PDV uključen u cijenu?** yeh lih doh·roo·chahk/peh·deh·veh oo·klyoo·chehn oo tsih·yeh·noo |
| Are there any discounts? | **Ima li popusta?** ih·mah lih poh·poo·stah |

## Preferences

| Can I see the room? | **Mogu li vidjeti sobu?** moh·goo lih vih·dyeh·tih soh·boo |
| I'd like...room. | **Htio m/Htjela f bih...sobu.** htih·oh/htyeh·lah bih...soh·boo |
| a better | **bolju** boh·lyoo |
| a bigger | **veću** veh·choo |
| a cheaper | **jeftiniju** yeh·ftih·nih·yoo |
| a quieter | **mirniju** mihr·nih·yoo |
| I'll take it. | **Uzimam.** oo·zih·mahm |
| No, I won't take it. | **Ne, neću je uzeti.** neh neh·choo yeh oo·zeh·tih |

## Questions

| Where's...? | **Gdje je...?** gdyeh yeh... |
| the bar | **bar** bahr |
| the bathroooms | **zahod** zah·hohd |
| the elevator [lift] | **lift** lihft |
| the pool | **bazen** bah·zehn |
| Can I have...? | **Mogu li dobiti...?** moh·goo lih doh·bih·tih... |
| a blanket | **deku** deh·koo |
| an iron | **glačalo** glah·chah·loh |

| the room key/ key card | **ključ/karticu od sobe** *klyooch/kahr·tih·tsoo ohd soh·beh* |
| a pillow | **jastuk** *jah·stook* |
| soap | **sapun** *sah·poon* |
| toilet paper | **toaletni papir** *toh·ah·leh·tnih pah·pihr* |
| a towel | **ručnik** *roo·chnihk* |
| Do you have an adapter for this? | **Imate li adapter za ovo?** *ih·mah·teh lih ah·dah·ptehr zah oh·voh* |
| How do I turn on the lights? | **Kako se pali svjetlo?** *kah·koh seh pah·lih svyeh·tloh* |
| Can you wake me at…? | **Možete li me probuditi u…?** *moh·zheh·teh lih meh proh·boo·dih·tih oo…* |
| When does breakfast start/end? | **Kada počinje/završava doručak?** *kah·dah poh·chih·nyeh/zah·vr·shah·vah doh·roo·chahk* |
| Can I leave this in the safe? | **Mogu li ostaviti ovo u sefu?** *moh·goo lih oh·stah·vih·tih oh·voh oo seh·foo* |
| Can I have my things from the safe? | **Mogu li dobiti svoje stvari iz sefa?** *moh·goo lih doh·bih·tih svoh·yeh stvah·rih ihz seh·fah* |
| Is there mail [post]/ a message for me? | **Ima li pošte/poruka za mene?** *ih·mah lih poh·shteh/poh·roo·kah zah meh·neh* |
| Do you have a laundry service? | **Imate li uslugu pranja rublja?** *ih·mah·teh lih oo·sloo·goo prah·nyah roo·blyah* |

## YOU MAY SEE...

| | |
|---|---|
| **GURAJ/POVUCI** | push/pull |
| **ZAHOD** | restroom [toilet] |
| **TUŠEVI** | showers |
| **LIFT** | elevator [lift] |
| **STEPENICE** | stairs |
| **LEDOMATI** | ice machines |
| **AUTOMATI** | vending machines |
| **PRAONICA** | laundry |
| **NE SMETAJ** | do not disturb |
| **POŽARNI IZLAZ** | fire door |
| **IZLAZ (U SLUČAJU OPASNOSTI)** | [emergency] exit |
| **POZIV ZA BUĐENJE** | wake-up call |

## Problems

| | |
|---|---|
| There's a problem. | **Ima jedan problem.** *ih·mah yeh·dahn proh·blehm* |
| I lost my key/key card. | **Izgubio *m*/Izgubila *f* sam ključ/karticu od sobe.** *ihz·goo·bih·oh/ihz·goo·bih·lah sahm klyooch/ kahr·tih·tsoo ohd soh·beh* |
| I'm locked out of the room. | **Ostao sam zaključan *m*/Ostala sam zaključana *f* van sobe.** *oh·stah·oh sahm zah·klyoo·chahn/oh·stah·lah sahm zah·klyoo·chah·nah vahn soh·beh* |
| There's no hot water/ toilet paper. | **Nema tople vode/toaletnog papira.** *neh·mah toh·pleh voh·deh/toh·ah·leh·tnohg pah·pih·reh* |
| The room is dirty. | **Soba je prljava.** *soh·bah yeh pr·lyah·vah* |
| There are bugs in the room. | **U sobi ima buba.** *oo soh·bih ih·mah boo·bah* |
| ...doesn't work. | **...ne radi.** *... neh rah·dih* |
| Can you fix...? | **Možete li popraviti...?** *moh·zheh·teh lih poh·prah·vih·tih...* |

| the air conditioning | **klima-uređaj** *klih·mah oo·reh·jahy* |
| the fan | **ventilator** *vehn·tih·lah·tor* |
| the heat [heating] | **grijanje** *grih·yah·nyeh* |
| the light | **svjetlo** *svyeh·tloh* |
| the TV | **televizor** *teh·leh·vih·zohr* |
| the toilet | **zahod** *zah·hohd* |
| I'd like another room. | **Htio** *m*/**Htjela** *f* **bih drugu sobu.** |
| | *htih·oh/htyeh·lah bih droo·goo soh·boo* |

Voltage in Croatia is 220 volts at the frequency of 50 Hz.

## Checking Out

| When's check-out? | **Kada moramo napusiti?** |
| | *kah·dah moh·rah·moh nah·poo·stih·tih* |
| Can I leave my bags here until...? | **Mogu li ostaviti torbe ovdje dok...?** |
| | *moh·goo lih oh·stah·vih·tih tohr·beh ohv·dyeh dohk...* |
| Can I have a bill/ an itemized receipt? | **Mogu li dobiti detaljan račun/priznanicu?** |
| | *moh·goo lih doh·bih·tih deh·tah·lyahn rah·choon/ prih·znah·nih·tsoo* |
| I think there's a mistake. | **Mislim da je to greška.** |
| | *mih·slihm dah yeh toh greh·shkah* |
| I'll pay in cash/by credit card. | **Platit ću gotovinom/kreditnom karticom.** *plah·tiht choo goh·toh·vih·nohm/kreh·dih·tnohm kahr·tih·tsohm* |

Tipping hotel staff such as the concierge, porters and housekeeping, is customary in Croatia. Generally, small change is acceptable per service rendered.

## Renting

| | |
|---|---|
| I've reserved an apartment/a room. | **Rezervirao** *m*/**Rezervirala** *f* **sam apartman/sobu.** *reh·zehr·vih·rah·oh/reh·zehr·vih·rah·lah sahm ah·pahrt·mahn/soh·boo* |
| My name is… | **Moje ime je…** *moh·yeh ih·meh yeh…* |
| Can I have the key/ key card? | **Mogu li dobiti ključ/karticu?** *moh·goo lih doh·bih·tih klyooch/kahr·tih·tsoo* |
| Are there…? | **Ima li…?** *ih·mah lih…* |
| dishes | **posuđa** *poh·soo·jah* |
| pillows | **jastuka** *yah·stoo·kah* |
| sheets | **plahti** *plah·htee* |
| towels | **ručnika** *roo·chnih·kah* |
| utensils | **pribor za jelo** *prih·bohr zah yeh·loh* |
| When do I put out the bins/recycling? | **Kada iznosim smeće/reciklažu?** *kah·dah ihz·noh·sihm smeh·cheh/reh·tsih·klah·zhoo* |
| …is broken. | **…je pokvaren.** *…yeh poh·kvah·rehn* |
| How does…work? | **Kako radi…?** *kah·koh rah·dih…* |
| the air conditioner | **klima-uređaj** *klih·mah oo·reh·jahy* |
| the dishwasher | **perilica za posuđe** *peh·rih·lih·tsah zah poh·soo·jeh* |
| the freezer | **zamrzivač** *zah·mr·zih·vahch* |
| the heater | **grijanje** *grih·yah·nyeh* |

| the microwave | **mikrovalna** *mih·kroh·vahl·nah* |
| the refrigerator | **hladnjak** *hlah·dnyahk* |
| the stove | **štednjak** *shteh·dnyahk* |
| the washing machine | **perilica** *peh·rih·lih·tsah* |

For Oven Temperatures, see page 174.

## Domestic Items

| I need… | **Treba mi…** *treh·bah mih…* |
| an adapter | **adapter** *ah·dah·ptehr* |
| aluminum [kitchen] foil | **aluminijska folija** *ah·loo·mih·nihy·skah foh·lih·yah* |
| a bottle opener | **otvarač za boce** *oh·tvah·rahch zah boh·tseh* |
| a broom | **metla** *meh·tlah* |
| a can opener | **otvarač za konzerve** *oh·tvah·rahch zah kohn·zehr·veh* |
| cleaning supplies | **sredstvo za čišćenje** *srehd·stvoh zah chihsh·cheh·nyeh* |
| a corkscrew | **vadičep** *vah·dih·chehp* |
| detergent | **deterdžent** *deh·tehr·jehnt* |
| dishwashing liquid | **deterdžent za posuđe** *deh·tehr·jehnt zah poh·soo·jeh* |
| bin bags | **vrećice za smeće** *vreh·chih·tseh zah smeh·cheh* |
| a lightbulb | **žarulja** *zhah·roo·lyah* |
| matches | **žigice** *zhih·gih·tseh* |
| a mop | **krpa za pod** *kr·pah zah pohd* |
| napkins | **salveta** *sahl·veh·tah* |
| paper towels | **ubrus** *oo·broos* |
| plastic wrap [cling film] | **prozirna plastična folija** *proh·zihr·nah plah·stih·chnah foh·lih·yah* |
| a plunger | **odčepljivač odvoda** *ohd·cheh·plyih·vahch ohd·voh·dah* |
| scissors | **škare** *shkah·reh* |
| a vacuum cleaner | **usisavač** *oo·sih·sah·vahch* |

For In the Kitchen, see page 78.

## At the Hostel

| | |
|---|---|
| Is there a bed available? | **Ima li slobodan krevet?** ih·mah lih sloh·boh·dahn kreh·veht |
| Can I have…? | **Mogu li dobiti…?** moh·goo lih doh·bih·tih… |
| a single/ double room | **jednokrevetnu/dvokrevetnu sobu** yeh·dnoh·kreh·veh·tnoo/dvoh·kreh·veh·tnoo soh·boo |
| Can I have…? | **Mogu li dobiti…?** moh·goo lih doh·bih·tih… |
| a blanket | **deku** deh·koo |
| a pillow | **jastuk** yah·stook |
| sheets | **plahte** plah·hteh |
| a towel | **ručnik** roo·chnihk |
| Do you have lockers? | **Imate li ormariće?** ih·mah·teh lih ohr·mah·rih·cheh |
| When do you lock up? | **Kada zaključavate?** kah·dah zah·klyoo·chah·vah·teh |
| Do I need a membership card? | **Treba li mi članska iskaznica?** treh·bah lih mih chlahn·skah ihs·kah·znih·tsah |
| Here's my International Student Card. | **Ovo je moja međunarodna studentska iskaznica.** oh·voh yeh moh·yah meh·joo·nah·roh·dnah stoo·dehn·tskah ihs·kah·znih·tsah |

Croatian youth hostels are well situated throughout the country and generally offer quality, inexpensive, clean and comfortable accommodation. Backpackers, families, students, members of Hostelling International and non-members are all welcome.

## Going Camping

| | |
|---|---|
| Can I camp here? | **Mogu li ovdje kampirati?** moh·goo lih ohv·dyeh kahm·pih·rah·tih |
| Where's the campsite? | **Gdje je kamp?** gdyeh yeh kahmp |

| | |
|---|---|
| What is the charge per day/week? | **Koja je cijena po danu/tjednu?** *koh·yah yeh cih·yeh·nah poh dah·noo/tyeh·dnoo* |
| Are there…? | **Postoji li…?** *poh·stoh·yih lih…* |
| cooking facilities | **mogućnost kuhanja** *moh·gooch·nohst koo·hah·nyah* |
| electric outlets | **utičnica** *oo·tih·chnih·tsah* |
| laundry facilitie | **mogućnost pranja veša** *moh·gooch·nohst prah·nyah veh·shah* |
| showers | **tuš** *toosh* |
| tents for rent [hire] | **šator za iznajmljivanje** *shah·tohr zah ihz·nahy·mlyih·vah·nyeh* |
| Where can I empty the chemical toilet? | **Gdje mogu isprazniti kemijski zahod?** *gdyeh moh·goo ihz·prah·znih·tih keh·mihy·skih zah·hohd* |

For Domestic Items, see page 46.

---

**YOU MAY SEE…**

| | |
|---|---|
| **PITKA VODA** | drinking water |
| **ZABRANJENO KAMPIRANJE** | no camping |
| **ZABRANJENO PALJENJE VATRE/ROŠTILJANJE** | no fires/barbecues |

## ESSENTIAL

| | |
|---|---|
| Where's an internet cafe? | **Gdje ima internet cafe?** _gdyeh ih·mah ihn·tehr·neht kah·feh_ |
| Can I access the internet/check email? | **Mogu li pristupiti internetu/provjeriti e-mail?** _moh·goo lih prih·stoo·pih·tih ihn·tehr·neh·too/ proh·vyeh·rih·tih ee·mehyl_ |
| How much per hour/ half hour? | **Koliko košta po satu/pola sata?** _koh·lih·koh koh·shtah poh sah·too/poh·lah sah·tah_ |
| How do I connect/ log on? | **Kako se konektiram/logiram?** _kah·koh seh koh·neh·ktih·rahm/loh·gih·rahm_ |
| A phone card, please. | **Telefonsku karticu, molim Vas.** _teh·leh·fohn·skoo kahr·tih·tsoo moh·lihm vahs_ |
| Can I have your phone number? | **Mogu li dobiti vaš broj telefona?** _moh·goo lih doh·bih·tih vahsh brohy teh·leh·foh·nah_ |
| Here's my number/ email. | **To je moj broj/e-mail.** _toh yeh mohy brohy/ee·mehyl_ |
| Call me. | **Nazovite me.** _nah·zoh·vih·teh meh_ |
| Email me. | **Napišite mi e-mail.** _nah·pih·shih·teh mih ee·mehyl_ |
| Hello. This is… | **Halo. Pri telefonu…** _hah·loh prih teh·leh·foh·noo…_ |
| Can I speak to…? | **Mogu li razgovarati s…?** _moh·goo lih rahz·goh·vah·rah·tih s…_ |
| Can you repeat that? | **Možete li ponoviti?** _moh·zheh·teh lih poh·noh·vih·tih_ |
| I'll call back later. | **Nazvat ću kasnije.** _nah·zvaht choo kah·snih·yeh_ |
| Bye. | **Doviđenja.** _doh·vih·jeh·nyah_ |
| Where's the post office? | **Gdje je pošta?** _gdyeh yeh poh·shtah_ |
| I'd like to send this to… | **Htio m/Htjela f bih poslati ovo u…** _htih·oh/htyeh·lah bih poh·slah·tih oh·voh oo…_ |

## Online

| | |
|---|---|
| Where's an internet cafe? | **Gdje ima internet cafe?** |
| | *gdyeh ih·mah ihn·tehr·neht kah·feh* |
| Does it have wireless internet? | **Ima li bežični internet?** |
| | *ih·mah lih beh·zhih·chnih ihn·tehr·neht* |
| What is the WiFi password? | **Koja je lozinka za bežičnu mrežu?** |
| | *koh·yah yeh loh·zihn·kah zah beh·zhih·chnoo mreh·zhoo* |
| Is the WiFi free? | **Je li bežična mreža besplatna?** |
| | *yeh lih beh·zhih·chnah mreh·zhah behs·plaht·nah* |
| Do you have bluetooth? | **Imate li bluetooth?** *ih·mah·teh lih bloo·tooth* |
| How do I turn the computer on/off? | **Kako uključivam/gasim računar?** |
| | *kah·koh oo·klyoo·chih·vahm/gah·sihm rah·choo·nahr* |
| Can I...? | **Mogu li...?** *moh·goo lih...* |
| use any computer | **koristiti bilo koji računar** |
| | *koh·rih·stih·tih bih·loh koh·yih rah·choo·nahr* |
| access the internet | **pristupiti internetu** *prih·stoo·pih·tih ihn·tehr·neh·too* |
| check my email | **provjeriti e-mail** *proh·vyeh·rih·tih ee·mehyl* |
| print | **printati** *prihn·tah·tih* |
| plug in/charge my laptop/iPhone/iPad/BlackBerry? | **uključiti/napuniti svoj laptop/iPhone/iPad?** |
| | *ook·lyoo·chih·tih/nah·puh·nih·tih svohy lap·top/i·phone/i·pad* |
| access Skype? | **Mogu li koristiti Skype?** |
| | *moh·goo lih koh·rih·stih·tee skype* |
| How much per hour/half hour? | **Koliko košta po satu/pola sata?** |
| | *koh·lih·koh koh·shtah poh sah·too/poh·lah sah·tah* |
| How do I...? | **Kako se...?** *kah·koh seh...* |
| connect/disconnect | **konektiram/diskonektiram** |
| | *koh·neh·ktih·rahm/dis·koh·neh·ktih·rahm* |
| log on/off | **logiram/odlogiram** *loh·gih·rahm/od·loh·gih·rahm* |
| type this symbol | **tipka ovaj znak** *tihp·kah oh·vahy znahk* |

| What's your email? | **Koja je vaša e-mail adresa?** |
| | *koh·yah yeh vah·shah ee·mehyl ah·dreh·sah* |
| My email is… | **Moja e-mail adresa je…** |
| | *moh·yah ee·mehyl ah·dreh·sah yeh…* |
| Do you have a scanner? | **Imate li skener?** *ih·mah·teh lih skeh·nehr* |

## Social Media

| Are you on Facebook/ | **Jesi li na Facebooku/Twitteru?** |
| Twitter? | *yeh·sih lih nah fehys·boo·koo/twih·teh·roo* |
| What's your username? | **Koje ti je korisničko ime?** |
| | *koh·yeh tih yeh koh·rihs·nihch·koh ihmeh* |
| I'll add you as a friend. | **Dodat ću te za prijatelja.** |
| | *doh·daht choo teh zah prih·ya·teh·lya* |
| I'll follow you on | **Slijedit ću te na Twitteru.** |
| Twitter. | *slih·yeh·diht choo teh nah twih·teh·roo* |
| Are you following…? | **Slijediš li…?** *slih·yeh·dish lih* |
| I'll put the pictures on | **Stavit ću slike na Facebook/Twitter.** |
| Facebook/Twitter. | *stah·viht choo slih·keh nah fehys·book/twih·tehr* |
| I'll tag you in the | **Tagirat ću te na slikama.** |
| pictures. | *tah·gih·raht choo teh nah slih·kah·mah* |

## Phone

| A phone card/prepaid | **Telefonsku karticu/Prepaid telefon, molim Vas.** |
| phone, please. | *teh·leh·fohn·skoo kahr·tih·tsoo/prih·pehyd teh·leh·fohn* |
| | *moh·lihm vahs* |
| How much? | **Koliko?** *koh·lih·koh* |
| Can I recharge/buy | **Mogu li napuniti/kupiti nadoplatni bon za ovaj** |
| minutes for this | **telefon?** *moh·goo lih nah·poo·nih·tih/koo·pih·tih* |
| phone? | *nah·doh·plah·tnih bohn zah oh·vahy teh·leh·fohn* |
| Where's the pay | **Gdje je telefonska govornica?** |
| phone? | *gdyeh yeh teh·leh·fohn·skah goh·vohr·nih·tsah* |

## YOU MAY SEE...

| | |
|---|---|
| **ZATVORI** | close |
| **BRIŠI** | delete |
| **E-MAIL** | email |
| **IZLAZ** | exit |
| **POMOĆ** | help |
| **MESSENGER** | instant messenger |
| **INTERNET** | internet |
| **LOGIN** | login |
| **NOVA (PORUKA)** | new message |
| **UKLJUČENO/ISKLJUČENO** | on/off |
| **OTVORI** | open |
| **ISPIS** | print |
| **ŠALJI** | send |
| **SAČUVAJ** | save |
| **KORISNIČKO IME/LOZINKA** | username/password |
| **BEŽIČNI INTERNET** | wireless internet |

| | |
|---|---|
| What's the area/ country code for...? | **Koji je regionalni/državni pozivni broj za...?** *koh·yih yeh reh·gih·oh·nahl·nih/dr·zhah·vnih poh·zih·vnih brohy zah...* |
| What's the number for Information? | **Koji je broj informacija?** *koh·yih yeh brohy ihn·fohr·mah·tsih·yah* |
| I'd like the number for... | **Htio** *m*/**Htjela** *f* **bih broj za...** *htih·oh/htyeh·lah bih brohy zah...* |
| I'd like to call collect [reverse the charges]. | **Htio** *m*/**Htjela** *f* **bih nazvati na račun primatelja poziva.** *htih·oh/htyeh·lah bih nah·zvah·tih nah rah·choon prih·mah·teh·lyah poh·zih·vah* |
| My phone doesn't work here. | **Moj telefon ne radi ovdje.** *mohy teh·leh·fohn neh rah·dih ohv·dyeh* |

| | |
|---|---|
| What network are you on? | **Na kojoj si mreži?** *nah koh·yohy sih mreh·zhih* |
| Is it 3G? | **Je li to 3G?** *yeh lih toh t·ree geh* |
| I have run out of credit/minutes. | **Nemam više kredita/minuta.** *neh·mahm vih·sheh kreh·dih·tah/mih·noo·tah* |
| Can I buy some credit? | **Mogu li kupiti nadoplatni bon?** *moh·goo lih koo·pih·tih nah·doh·plah·tnih bohn* |
| Do you have a phone charger? | **Imate li punjač za mobitel?** *ih·mah·teh lih poo·nyach zah moh·bih·tehl* |
| Can I have your number? | **Mogu li dobiti vaš broj?** *moh·goo lih doh·bih·tih vahsh brohy* |
| Here's my number. | **To je moj broj.** *toh yeh mohy brohy* |
| Please call/text me. | **Molim Vas nazovite me/napišite mi poruku.** *moh·lihm vahs nah·zoh·vih·teh meh/nah·pih·shih·teh mih poh·roo·koo* |
| I'll call you. | **Nazvat ću Vas.** *nah·zvaht choo vahs* |
| I'll text you. | **Napisat ću Vam poruku.** *nah·pih·saht choo vahm poh·roo·koo* |

For Numbers, see page 169.

## Telephone Etiquette

| | |
|---|---|
| Hello. This is... | **Halo. Pri telefonu...** *hah·loh prih teh·leh·foh·noo...* |
| Can I speak to...? | **Mogu li razgovarati s...?** *moh·goo lih rah·zgoh·vah·rah·tih s* |
| Extension... | **Lokalni broj...** *loh·kahl·nih brohy* |
| Speak louder/more slowly, please. | **Govorite glasnije/sporije, molim Vas.** *goh·voh·rih·teh glah·snih·yeh/spoh·rih·yeh moh·lihm vahs* |
| Can you repeat that? | **Možete li to ponoviti?** *moh·zheh·teh lih toh poh·noh·vih·tih* |
| I'll call back later. | **Nazvat ću kasnije.** *nah·zvaht choo kah·snih·yeh* |
| Bye. | **Doviđenja.** *doh·vih·jeh·nyah* |

## YOU MAY HEAR...

**Tko zove?** *tkoh zoh·veh* — Who's calling?

**Pričekajte.** *prih·cheh·kahy·teh* — Hold on.

**Spojit ću Vas.** *spoh·yiht choo vahs* — I'll put you through to him/her.

**On/Ona nije tu/je na drugoj vezi.**
*ohn/oh·na nih·yeh too/yeh nah droo·gohy veh·zih* — He/She is not here/on another line.

**Želite li ostaviti poruku?**
*zheh·lih·teh lih oh·stah·vih·tih poh·roo·koo* — Would you like to leave a message?

**Nazovite kasnije/za deset minuta.**
*nah·zoh·vih·teh kah·snih·yeh zah deh·seht mih·noo·tah* — Call back later/in 10 minutes.

**Može li Vas on/ona nazvati?**
*moh·zheh lih vahs ohn/oh·na nah·zvah·tih* — Can he/she call you back?

**Koji je vaš broj?** *koh·yih yeh vash brohy* — What's your number?

## Fax

Can I send/receive a fax here? — **Mogu li ovdje poslati/primiti faks?** *moh·goo lih ohv·dyeh poh·slah·tih/prih·mih·tih fahks*

What's the fax number? — **Koji je broj faksa?** *koh·yih yeh brohy fah·ksah*

**Telefonske govornice** (pay phones) in Croatia are card operated; phone cards can be purchased from post offices, newsstands and tobacconists. Post offices also have phone booths from which calls can be made. Payment is made when the call is complete. To call the U.S. or Canada dial 00 + 1 + area code + phone number. To call the U.K., dial 00 + 44 + area code + phone number.

| Please fax this to… | **Molim Vas faksirajte ovo na…** |
| | *moh·lihm vahs fah·ksih·rahy·teh oh·voh nah…* |

## Post

| Where's the post office/ | **Gdje je pošta/poštanski ormarić?** *gdyeh yeh* |
| mailbox [postbox]? | *poh·shtah/poh·shtahn·skih ohr·mah·rihch* |
| A stamp for this | **Poštansku markicu za ovu razglednicu/ovo pismo** |
| postcard/letter to… | **do…** *poh·shtahn·skoo mahr·kih·tsoo zah oh·voo* |
| | *rahz·gleh·dnih·tsoo/oh·voh pee·smoh doh…* |
| How much? | **Koliko?** *koh·lih·koh* |
| Send this package by | **Pošaljite taj paket avionskom/express poštom.** |
| airmail/express. | *poh·shah·lyih·teh tahy pah·keht ah·vih·ohn·skohm/* |
| | *ehks·prehs poh·shtohm* |
| A receipt, please. | **Račun, molim Vas.** *rah·choon moh·lihm vahs* |

### YOU MAY HEAR…

| **Popunite obrazac za carinsku deklaraciju.** | Can you fill out the |
| *poh·poo·nih·teh oh·brah·zahts zah tsah·rihn·skoo* | customs declaration |
| *deh·klah·rah·tsih·yoo* | form? |
| **Koja je vrijednost?** *koh·yah yeh vrih·yehd·nohst* | What's the value? |
| **Što je unutra?** *shtoh yeh oo·noo·trah* | What's inside? |

**Pošta** (post offices) are generally open from 7:00 a.m. to 7:00 p.m. weekdays and from 7:00 a.m. to 1:00 p.m. on Saturdays. In larger cities and tourist destinations, post offices may stay open until 10:00 p.m. and also open on Sundays.

# Food & Drink

## ESSENTIAL

| | |
|---|---|
| Can you recommend a good restaurant/bar? | **Možete li preporučiti dobar restoran/bar?** *moh·zheh·teh lih preh·poh·roo·chih·tih doh·bahr reh·stoh·rahn/bahr* |
| Is there a traditional Croatian/an inexpensive restaurant nearby? | **Ima li blizu tradicionalni hrvatski/jeftin restoran?** *ih·mah lih blih·zoo trah·dih·tsih·oh·nahl·nih hr·vah·tskih/yehf·tihn reh·stoh·rahn* |
| A table for..., please. | **Stol za jednu osobu/dvoje, molim Vas.** *stohl zah yeh·dnoo oh·soh·boo/dvoh·yeh moh·lihm vahs* |
| Can we sit...? | **Možemo li sjesti...?** *moh·zheh·moh lih syeh·stih...* |
| here/there | **ovdje/tamo** *ohv·dyeh/tah·moh* |
| outside | **vani** *vah·nih* |
| in a non-smoking area | **u prostor za nepušače** *oo proh·stohr zah neh·poo·shah·cheh* |
| I'm waiting for someone. | **Čekam nekoga.** *cheh·kahm neh·koh·gah* |
| Where are the toilets? | **Gdje je zahod?** *gdyeh yeh zah·hohd* |
| A menu, please. | **Jelovnik, molim Vas.** *jeh·loh·vnihk moh·lihm vahs* |
| What do you recommend? | **Što preporučate?** *shtoh preh·poh·roo·chah·teh* |
| I'd like... | **Htio *m*/Htjela *f* bih...** *htih·oh/htyeh·lah bih...* |
| Some more..., please. | **Još malo..., molim Vas.** *johsh mah·loh... moh·lihm vahs* |
| Enjoy your meal! | **Dobar tek!** *doh·bahr tehk* |
| The check [bill], please | **Račun, molim Vas.** *rah·choon moh·lihm vahs* |
| Is service included? | **Je li usluga uračunata u cijenu?** *yeh lih oo·sloo·gah oo·rah·choo·nah·tah oo cih·yeh·noo* |

| Can I pay by credit card/have a receipt? | **Mogu li platiti kreditnom karticom/dobiti račun?** moh·goo lih plah·tih·tih kreh·diht·nohm kahr·tih·tsohm/doh·bih·tih rah·choon |
| Thank you. | **Hvala Vam!** hvah·lah vahm |

## Where to Eat

| Can you recommend...? | **Možete li preporučiti…?** moh·zheh·teh lih preh·poh·roo·chih·tih… |
| a restaurant | **restoran** reh·stoh·rahn |
| a bar | **bar** bahr |
| a cafe | **kavanu** kah·vah·noo |
| a fast-food place | **fast food** fahst food |
| a cheap restaurant | **jeftin restoran** yehf·tihn reh·stoh·rahn |
| an expensive restaurant | **skup restoran** skoop reh·stoh·rahn |
| a restaurant with a good view | **restoran s dobrim pogledom** reh·stoh·rahn s doh·brihm poh·gleh·dohm |
| an authentic/a non-touristy restaurant | **autentičan restoran/restoran koji nije pun turista** aooteh·ntih·chahn reh·stoh·rahn/reh·stoh·rahn koh·yih nih·yeh puhn too·rihstah |

## Reservations & Preferences

| I'd like to reserve a table... | **Htio** m/**Htjela** f **bih… rezervirati stol…** htih·oh/htyeh·lah bih reh·zehr·vih·rah·tih stohl… |
| for two | **za dvije osobe** zah dvih·yeh oh·soh·beh |
| for this evening | **za večeras** zah veh·cheh·rahs |
| for tomorrow at... | **za sutra u…sati** zah soo·trah oo…sah·tih |
| A table for two, please. | **Stol za dvoje, molim Vas.** stohl zah dvoh·yeh moh·lihm vahs |
| We have a reservation. | **Rezervirali smo.** reh·zehr·vih·rah·lih smoh |

## YOU MAY HEAR...

**Jeste li rezervirali?**
*yeh·steh lih reh·zehr·vih·rah·lih*

Do you have a
reservation?

**Koliko osoba?** *koh·lih·koh oh·soh·bah*

How many?

**Za pušače ili za nepušače?**
*zah poo·shah·cheh ih·lih zah neh·poo·shah·cheh*

Smoking or
non-smoking?

**Jeste li se odlučili?**
*yeh·steh lih seh oh·dloo·chih·lih*

Are you ready to order?

**Što želite?** *shtoh zheh·lih·teh*

What would you like?

**Preporučujem...** *preh·poh·roo·choo·yehm...*

I recommend...

**Dobar tek.** *doh·bahr tehk*

Enjoy your meal.

| | |
|---|---|
| I have a reservation. | **Imam rezervaciju.** |
| | *ih·mahm reh·zehr·vah·tsih·yoo* |
| My name is... | **Na ime...** *nah ih·meh...* |
| Can we sit...? | **Možemo li sjesti...?** *moh·zheh·moh lih syeh·stih...* |
| here/there | **ovdje/tamo** *ohv·dyeh/tah·moh* |
| outside | **vani** *vah·nih* |

| in a non-smoking area | **u prostor za nepušače** *oo proh·stohr zah neh·poo·shah·cheh* |
| by the window | **pokraj prozora** *poh·krahy proh·zoh·rah* |
| in the shade | **u sjenu** *oo syeh·noo* |
| in the sun | **na sunce** *nah soon·tseh* |
| Where's the restroom [toilet]? | **Gdje je zahod?** *gdyeh yeh zah·hohd* |

## How to Order

| Waiter/Waitress! | **Konobar!** *koh·noh·bahr* |
| We're/I'm ready to order. | **Naručio** *m*/**Naručila** *f* **bih.** *nah·roo·chih·oh/nah·roo·chih·lah bih* |
| May I see the wine list? | **Vinsku kartu, molim Vas.** *vihn·skoo kahr·too moh·lihm vahs* |
| I'd like… | **Htio** *m*/**Htjela** *f* **bih…** *htih·oh/htyeh·lah bih…* |
| a bottle of… | **bocu…** *boh·tsoo…* |
| a carafe of… | **vrč…** *vrch…* |
| a glass of… | **čašu…** *chah·shoo…* |
| The menu, please. | **Jelovnik, molim Vas.** *jeh·loh·vnihk moh·lihm vahs* |
| Do you have…? | **Imate li…?** *ih·mah·teh lih…* |

| a menu in English | **jelovnik na engleskom** |
| | *jeh·loh·vnihk nah ehn·gleh·skoh·meh* |
| a fixed-price menu | **fiksni meni** *fihk·snih meh·nih* |
| a children's menu | **meni za djecu** *meh·nee zah dyeh·tsoo* |
| What do you recommend? | **Što preporučujete?** |
| | *shtoh preh·poh·roo·cho·yeh·teh* |
| What's this? | **Što je to?** *sthoh yeh toh* |
| What's in it? | **Što je unutra?** *shtoh yeh oo·noo·trah* |
| I'd like… | **Htio** m/**Htjela** f **bih…** *htih·oh/htyeh·lah bih…* |
| More…, please. | **Još…, molim Vas.** *johsh…moh·lihm vahs* |
| With/Without… | **Sa/Bez…** *sah/behz…* |
| I can't have… | **Ne jedem…** *neh yeh·dehm…* |
| I can't eat… | **Ne mogu jesti…** *neh·moh·goo yeh·stih* |
| rare | **sirov** *sih·rohv* |
| medium | **srednje pečen** *srehd·nyeh peh·chehn* |
| well-done | **dobro pečen** *doh·broh peh·chehn* |
| It's to go [take away]. | **To je za ponijeti.** *toh yeh zah poh·nih·yeh·tih* |
| please. | **Još…, molim Vas.** *johsh…moh·lihm vahs* |

61

**YOU MAY SEE…**

| (DNEVNI) MENI | menu (of the day) |
| USLUGA (NIJE) UKLJUČENA U CIJENU | service (not) included |
| DODATCI | specials |

## Cooking Methods

| baked | **pečen** *peh·chehn* |
| boiled (vegetables/meat) | **kuhan/na lešo** *koo·hahn/nah leh·shoh* |
| braised | **pirjan** *pihr·yahn* |

| breaded | **u kruhu** *oo kroo·hoo* |
| creamed | **u vrhnju** *oo vrh·nyoo* |
| diced | **sjeckan** *syeh·tskahn* |
| fileted | **rezan na filete** *reh·zahn nah fih·leh·teh* |
| fried | **pržen** *pr·zhehn* |
| grilled (vegetables/ fish) | **s roštilja/na gradele** *s roh·shtih·lyah/nah grah·deh·leh* |
| poached | **poširan** *poh·shie·rahn* |
| roasted | **pečen** *peh·chehn* |
| sautéed | **kratko pržen** *krah·tkoh pr·zhehn* |
| smoked | **dimljen** *dihm·lyehn* |
| steamed | **kuhan na pari** *koo·hahn nah pah·rih* |
| stewed | **baren** *bah·rehn* |
| stuffed | **punjen** *poo·nyehn* |

## Dietary Requirements

| I'm... | **Ja sam...** *yah sahm...* |
| diabetic | **dijabetičar** *dih·yah·beh·tih·chahr* |
| lactose intolerant | **osjetljiv** *m*/**osjetljiva** *f* **na laktozu** *oh·syeh·tlyihv/oh·syeh·tlyihvah nah lahk·toh·zoo* |
| vegetarian/vegan | **vegetarijanac/vegan** *veh·geh·tah·rih·yah·nats/veh·gahn* |
| I'm allergic to... | **Alergičan** *m*/**Alergična** *f* **sam...** *ah·lehr·gih·chahn/ah·lehr·gih·chnah sahm...* |
| I can't eat... | **Ne smijem jesti hranu koja sadrži...** *neh smih·yehm yeh·stih hrah·noo koh·yah sah·dr·zhih...* |
| dairy | **mlijeko** *mlih·yeh·koh* |
| gluten | **gluten** *gloo·tehn* |
| nuts | **orahe** *oh·rah·heh* |
| pork | **svinjetinu** *svih·nyeh·tih·noo* |
| shellfish | **školjke** *shkoh·lykeh* |

| | |
|---|---|
| spicy foods | **začinjenu hranu** |
| | *ah·chih·nyeh·noo hrah·noo* |
| wheat | **pšenicu** *psheh·nih·tsoo* |
| Is it halal/kosher? | **Je li to halal/košer?** |
| | *jeh lih toh hah·lahl/koh·shehr* |
| Do you have…? | **Imate li…?** *ih·mah·teh lih* |
| skimmed milk | **obrano mlijeko** *oh·brah·noh mlih·yeh·koh* |
| whole milk | **punomasno mlijeko** |
| | *puh·noh·mah·snoh mlih·yeh·koh* |
| soya milk | **sojino mlijeko** *soh·yee·noh mlih·yeh·koh* |

## Dining with Children

| | |
|---|---|
| Do you have children's portions? | **Imate li porcija za djecu?** *ih·mah·teh lih pohr·tsih·yah zah dyeh·tsoo* |
| Can I have a highchair/child's seat, please. | **Molim Vas visoku stolicu/stolicu za dijete.** *moh·lihm vahs vih·soh·koo stoh·lih·tsoo/stoh·lih·tsoo zah dyeh·teh* |
| Where can I feed/ change the baby? | **Gdje mogu nahraniti/presvući dijete?** *gdyeh moh·goo nah·hrah·nih·tih/preh·svoo·chih dih·yeh·teh* |
| Can you warm this? | **Možete li zagrijati ovo?** *moh·zheh·teh lih zah·grih·yah·tih oh·voh* |

For Traveling with Children, see page 143.

## How to Complain

| | |
|---|---|
| How much longer will our food be? | **Koliko dugo ćemo još čekati?** <br> *koh·lih·koh cheh·moh johsh cheh·kah·tih* |
| We can't wait any longer. | **Ne možemo više čekati.** <br> *neh moh·zheh·moh vih·sheh cheh·kah·tih* |
| We're leaving. | **Odlazimo.** *oh·dlah·zih·moh* |
| I didn't order this. | **Nisam to naručio *m*/naručila *f*.** <br> *nih·sahm toh nah·roo·chih·oh/nah·roo·chih·lah* |
| I ordered... | **Naručio *m*/Naručila *f* sam...** <br> *nah·roo·chih·oh/nah·roo·chih·lah sahm...* |
| I can't eat this. | **Ne mogu to pojesti.** *neh moh·goo toh poh·yeh·stih* |
| This is too... | **Ovo je...** *oh·voh yeh...* |
| cold/hot | **prehladno/prevruće** <br> *preh·hlah·dnoh/preh·vroo·cheh* |
| salty/spicy | **preslano/prezačinjeno** <br> *preh·slah·noh/preh·zah·chih·nyeh·noh* |

---

It is customary to tip about 10% of the total bill in restaurants. At bars, round up your bill to the nearest kuna/euro.

| | |
|---|---|
| tough/bland | **prežilavo/bezukusno** |
| | *preh·zhih·lah·voh/beh·zoo·koo·snoh* |
| This isn't clean/fresh. | **Ovo nije čisto/svježe.** |
| | *oh·voh nih·yeh chih·stoh/svyeh·zheh* |

## Paying

| | |
|---|---|
| The check [bill], please. | **Račun, molim Vas.** |
| | *rah·choon moh·lihm vahs* |
| Separate checks [bills], please. | **Zasebne račune, molim Vas.** |
| | *zah·seh·bneh rah·choo·neh moh·lihm vahs* |
| It's all together. | **Sve zajedno.** *sveh zah·yeh·dnoh* |
| Is service included? | **Je li usluga uračunata u cijenu?** |
| | *yeh lih oo·sloo·gah oo·rah·choo·nah·tah oo cih·yeh·noo* |
| What's this amount for? | **Što je uračunato u ovaj iznos?** |
| | *shtoh yeh oo·rah·choo·nah·toh oo oh·vahy ihz·nohs* |
| Can I have a receipt/ an itemized bill? | **Mogu li dobiti priznanicu/detaljan račun?** |
| | *moh·goo lih doh·bih·tih prih·znah·nih·tsoo/ deh·tah·lyahn rah·choon* |
| That was delicious! | **Bilo je ukusno!** *bih·loh yeh oo·koo·snoh* |
| I've already paid. | **Već sam platio/platila.** |
| | *vech sahm plah·tih·oh/plah·tih·lah* |

For Numbers, see page 169.

## Meals & Cooking

### Breakfast

| | |
|---|---|
| **hladni naresci** *hlah·dnih nah·rehs·tsih* | cold cuts [charcuterie] |
| **…jaje** *… yah·yeh* | …egg |
| **tvrdo kuhano** *tvr·doh koo·hah·noh* | hard-boiled |
| **meko kuhano** *meh·koh koo·hah·noh* | soft-boiled |
| **na oko** *nah oh·koh* | fried |
| **jogurt** *yoh·goort* | yogurt |
| **kava/čaj…** *kah·vah/chahy…* | coffee/tea… |
| **bez kofeina** *behz koh·feh·ih·nah* | decaf |
| **s mlijekom** *s mlih·yeh·kohm* | with milk |
| **sa šećerom sah** *sheh·cheh·rohm* | with sugar |
| **s umjetnim sladilom** *soo·myeh·tnihm slah·dih·lohm* | with artificial sweetener |
| **kajgana** *kahy·gah·nah* | scrambled egg |
| **kobasica** *koh·bah·sih·tsah* | sausage |
| **kroasan** *kroh·ah·sahn* | croissant |
| **kruh** *krooh* | bread |
| **maslac** *mah·slats* | butter |
| **mlijeko** *mlih·yeh·koh* | milk |
| **musli** *moo·slih* | granola [muesli] |
| **omlet** *ohm·leht* | omelet |
| **pecivo** *peh·tsih·voh* | roll |
| **pekmez/marmelada** *pehk·mehz/mahr·meh·lah·dah* | jam/jelly |
| **sir** *sihr* | cheese |

**slanina** *slah·nee·nah*     bacon
**sok od...** *sohk ohd...*     ...juice
**jabuke** *yah·boo·keh*     apple
**grejpa** *grehy·pah*     grapefruit
**naranče** *nah·tahn·cheh*     orange
**tost** *tohst*     toast
**voda** *voh·dah*     water
**zobena kaša**
*zoh·beh·nah kah·shah*     oatmeal
**(hladne/vruće) žitarice**     (cold/hot) cereal
*(hlah·dneh/vroo·cheh) zhih·tah·rih·tseh*

## Appetizers

**kulen** *koo·lehn*     sausage, spicy, flavored with
paprika (Slavonia)
**pohani sir** *poh·hah·nih sihr*     cheese, fried in breadcrumbs
**pršut i sir** *pr·shoot ih sihr*     smoked ham and cheese
**riblja pašteta** *rih·blyah pah·shteh·tah*     fish pâté
**rižot** *rih·zhoht*     risotto
**salata od hobotnice**     octopus salad
*sah·lah·ta ohd hoh·boh·tnih·tseh*
**slani inćuni** *slah·nih ihn·choo·nih*     salted anchovies

## Soup

| | |
|---|---|
| **grah** *grahh* | bean soup |
| **juha od gljiva** *yoo·hah ohd glyih·vah* | mushroom soup |
| **juha od rajčice** *yoo·hah ohd rahy·chih·tseh* | tomato soup |
| **pileća juha** *pih·leh·chah yoo·hah* | chicken soup |
| **povrtna juha** *poh·vr·tnah yoo·hah* | vegetable soup |
| **riblja juha** *rihb·lyah yoo·hah* | fish soup |

## Fish & Seafood

| | |
|---|---|
| **bakalar** *bah·kah·lahr* | cod |
| **brodet** *broh·deht* | fish stew |
| **haringa** *hah·rihn·gah* | herring |
| **hobotnica** *hoh·boh·tnih·tsah* | octopus |
| **iverak** *ih·veh·rahk* | halibut |
| **jastog** *yah·stohg* | lobster |
| **kamenica** *kah·meh·nih·tsah* | oyster |
| **kozice** *koh·zih·tseh* | shrimp |
| **lignje** *lihg·nyeh* | squid |
| **list** *lihst* | sole |

| | |
|---|---|
| **losos** *loh·sohs* | salmon |
| **lubin** *loo·bihn* | sea bass |
| **pastrva** *pah·str·vah* | trout |
| **rakovi** *rah·koh·vih* | crab |
| **sabljarka** *sahb·lyahr·kah* | swordfish |
| **školjke** *shkohly·keh* | clam |
| **tuna** *too·nah* | tuna |

Fish is traditionally prepared in two ways: **na gradele** (grilled) and **na lešo** (boiled). Grilled fish, usually salted and brushed with rosemary-infused olive oil, is cooked over a particular type of wood and aromatic herbs. The fish is then covered with finely grated parsley, garlic and oil, and usually served with vegetables or salad.

**Brodet** (fish stew) is prepared with different types of fish that are placed in a clay pot with garlic, parsley, laurel and tomatoes. The dish is usually served with polenta.

**Buzara** is popular along the Adriatic coastline. This shrimp, clam or mussel dish is prepared with olive oil, garlic, parsley and wine. It is often highly seasoned with a variety of aromatic spices.

## Meat & Poultry

| | |
|---|---|
| **čevapčići** *cheh·vahp·chih·chih* | rolls of ground meat, grilled |
| **govedina** *goh·veh·dih·nah* | beef |
| **janjetina** *jah·nyeh·tih·nah* | lamb |
| **jetrica** *yeh·trih·tsah* | liver |
| **kobasica** *koh·bah·sih·tsah* | sausage |
| **kunić** *koo·nihch* | rabbit |
| **odrezak** *oh·dreh·zahk* | steak |
| **pašticada** *pah·shtih·tsah·dah* | stewed beef with proscuitto, marinated in wine, lemon and rosemary |
| **patka** *pah·tkah* | duck |
| **piletina** *pih·leh·tih·nah* | chicken |
| **purica** *poo·rih·tsah* | turkey |
| **ražnjići** *rahzh·nyih·chih* | meat kebabs |
| **slanina** *slah·nih·nah* | bacon |
| **svinjetina** *svih·nyeh·tih·nah* | pork |
| **šunka** *shoon·kah* | ham |
| **teletina** *teh·leh·tih·nah* | veal |

Don't leave Croatia without trying at least one speciality dish such as: spit-roasted **janjetina** (lamb) or **pašticada** (see entry above) — a favorite Easter dish on the Dalmatian Coast. In northern Croatia, sample **Zagrebački odrezak** (veal steak stuffed with ham and cheese, and fried in breadcrumbs), **Zagorski kotlet** (beef cutlet with sausage, sauerkraut and boiled potatoes), turkey with **milnci** (thinly rolled pasta) and **kulen** (spicy sausage, flavored with paprika, typical in Slavonia).

## Vegetables & Staples

| | |
|---|---|
| **artičok** *ahr·tih·chohk* | artichoke |
| **avokado** *ah·voh·kah·doh* | avocado |
| **brokula** *broh·koo·lah* | broccoli |
| **češnjak** *cheh·shnyahk* | garlic |
| **gljive** *glyih·veh* | mushroom |
| **grah** *grahh* | beans |
| **grašak** *grah·shahk* | pea |
| **kukuruz** *koo·koo·rooz* | corn |
| **kupus** *koo·poos* | cabbage |
| **luk** *look* | onion |
| **mahune** *mah·hoo·neh* | green bean |
| **maslina** *mah·slih·nah* | olive |
| **mrkva** *mr·kvah* | carrot |
| **patlidžan** *pah·tlih·jahn* | eggplant [aubergine] |
| **šparoge** *shpah·roh·geh* | asparagus |
| **tjestenina** *tyeh·steh·nih·nah* | pasta |
| **zelena salata** *zeh·leh·nah sah·lah·tah* | lettuce |
| **krumpir** *kroom·pihr* | potato |
| **riža** *rih·zhah* | rice |

| | |
|---|---|
| **crvena/zelena paprika** *cr·veh·nah/zeh·leh·nah pah·prih·kah* | red/green pepper |
| **rajčica** *rahy·chih·tsah* | tomato |
| **špinat** *shih·naht* | spinach |
| **blitva** *bliht·vah* | Swiss chard |
| **povrće** *poh·vr·cheh* | vegetable |
| **tikvica** *tih·kvih·tsah* | zucchini [courgette] |

## Fruit

| | |
|---|---|
| **ananas** *ah·nah·nahs* | pineapple |
| **banana** *bah·nah·nah* | banana |
| **borovnica** *boh·roh·vnih·tsah* | blueberry |
| **breskva** *brehs·kvah* | peach |
| **dinja** *dih·nyah* | melon |
| **grejpfrut** *grehyp·froot* | grapefruit |
| **grožđe** *grohzh·jeh* | grape |
| **jabuka** *yah·boo·kah* | apple |
| **jagoda** *yah·goh·dah* | strawberry |
| **kruška** *kroo·shkah* | pear |
| **limeta** *lih·meh·tah* | lime |
| **limun** *lih·moon* | lemon |

| | |
|---|---|
| **lubenica** *loo·beh·nih·tsah* | watermelon |
| **malina** *mah·lih·nah* | raspberry |
| **mandarina** *mahn·dah·rih·nah* | tangerine |
| **marelica** *mah·reh·lih·tsah* | apricot |
| **naranča** *nah·rahn·chah* | orange |
| **smokva** *smoh·kvah* | fig |
| **šljiva** *shlyih·vah* | plum |
| **trešnja** *treh·shnyah* | cherry |
| **višnja** *vihsh·nyah* | sour cherry |
| **voćka** *voh·chkah* | fruit |

## Cheese

| | |
|---|---|
| **kozji sir** *koh·zyih sihr* | goat's cheese |
| **ovčiji sir** *ohv·chih·yih sihr* | sheep's cheese |
| **paški sir** *pahsh·kih sihr* | Pag cheese (hard, sheep's cheese from the island of Pag) |
| **sir sa plijesni** *sihr sah plih·yeh·snih* | blue cheese |
| **svježi sir** *svyeh·zhih sihr* | cream cheese |

## Dessert

| | |
|---|---|
| **fritule** *frih·too·leh* | fritters |
| **makovnjača** *mah·kohv·nyah·chah* | poppy seed roll |
| **orahnjača** *oh·rahh·nyah·chah* | walnut roll |
| **palačinka...** *pah·lah·chihn·kah...* | pancake... |
| **sa čokoladom i orasima** | with chocolate and walnuts |
| *sah choh·koh·lah·dohm ih oh·rah·sih·mah* | |
| **sa džemom** *sah jeh·mohm* | with jam |
| **sa sladoledom** *sah slah·doh·leh·dohm* | with ice cream |
| **rožata** *roh·zhah·tah* | crème caramel |

Typical desserts include **rožata** (crème caramel), **fritule** (fritters) and **palačinke** (thin pancakes, stuffed with various sweet fillings). In the summertime, fresh and tasty **sladoled** (ice cream) is very popular; flavors include: **čokolada** (chocolate), **lješnjak** (hazelnut), **orah** (walnut), **vanilija** (vanilla), **pistacija** (pistachio), **jagoda** (strawberry) and **višnja** (sour cherry).

**savijača od jabuka**
*sah·vih·yah·chah ohd yah·boo·kah*

apple strudel

**savijača od višanja**
*sah·vih·yah·chah ohd vih·shah·nyah*

sour cherry strudel

**sladoled** *slah·doh·lehd*

ice cream

## Sauces & Condiments

**kečap** *keh·chahp*

ketchup

**papar** *pah·pahr*

pepper

**senf** *sehnf*

mustard

**sol** *sohl*

salt

## At the Market

| | |
|---|---|
| WWhere are the carts [trolleys]/baskets? | **Gdje su kolica/košare?** *gdyeh soo koh·lih·tsah/koh·shahreh* |
| Where is…? | **Gdje je…?** *gdyeh yeh…* |
| I'd like some of that/this. | **Molim Vas malo ovog/tog.** *moh·lihm vahs mah·loh oh·vohg/tohg* |
| Can I taste it? | **Mogu li kušati to?** *moh·goo lih koo·shah·tih toh* |
| I'd like… | **Htio *m*/Htjela *f* bih…** *tih·oh/htyeh·lah bih…* |

| | | |
|---|---|---|
| a kilo/half-kilo of... | **kilo/pola kila...** | *kih·loh/poh·lah kih·lah...* |
| a liter of... | **litar...** | *lih·tahr...* |
| a piece of... | **komad...** | *koh·mahd...* |
| a slice of... | **krišku...** | *krih·shkooo...* |
| More./Less. | **Više./Manje.** | *vih·sheh/mah·nyeh* |
| How much? | **Koliko?** | *koh·lih·koh* |
| Where do I pay? | **Gdje plaćam?** | *gdyeh plah·chahm* |
| A bag, please. | **Vrećicu, molim Vas.** | |
| | *vreh·chih·tsoo moh·lihm vahs* | |
| I'm being helped. | **Već sam uslužen *m*/uslužena *f*.** | |
| | *vehch sahm oo·sloo·zhehn/oo·sloo·zheh·nah* | |

For Conversion Tables, see page 173.

Measurements in Europe are metric - and that applies to the weight of food too. If you tend to think in pounds and ounces, it's worth brushing up on what the metric equivalent is before you go shopping for fruit and veg in markets and supermarkets. Five hundred grams, or half a kilo, is a common quantity to order, and that converts to just over a pound (17.65 ounces, to be precise).

## YOU MAY HEAR...

**Mogu li Vam pomoći?**
*moh·goo lih vahm poh·moh·chih*

Can I help you?

**Što želite?** *shtoh zheh·lih·teh*

What would you like?

**Još nešto?** *johsh neh·shtoh*

Anything else?

**To je…kuna.** *toh yeh…koo·nah*

That's…kuna.

## YOU MAY SEE...

| | |
|---|---|
| UPOTRIJEBITI DO… | best if used by… |
| KALORIJA | calories |
| BEZ MASNOĆE | fat free |
| DRŽATI U HLADNJAKU | keep refrigerated |
| MOŽE SADRŽITI TRAGOVE | may contain traces of… |
| ZA MIKROVALNU | microwaveable |
| PRODAJE… | sell by… |
| ZA VEGETARIJANCE | suitable for vegetarians |

## In the Kitchen

| | | |
|---|---|---|
| bottle opener | **otvarač za boce** | *oh·tvah·rahch zah boh·tseh* |
| bowl | **zdjela** | *zdyeh·lah* |
| can opener | **otvarač za konzerve** | *oh·tvah·rahch zah kohn·zehr·veh* |
| corkscrew | **vadičep** | *vah·dih·chehp* |
| cup | **šalica** | *shah·lih·tsah* |
| fork | **vilica** | *vih·lih·tsah* |
| frying pan | **tava** | *tah·vah* |
| glass | **čaša** | *chah·shah* |
| (steak) knife | **nož (za odrezak)** | *nohzh (zah oh·dreh·zahk)* |
| measuring cup/spoon | **šalica/žlica za mjerenje** | |
| | *shah·lih·tsah/zhlih·tsah zah myeh·reh·nyeh* | |
| napkin | **ubrus** | *oo·broos* |
| plate | **tanjur** | *tah·nyoor* |
| pot | **lonac** | *loh·nahts* |
| spatula | **kuhača** | *koo·hah·chah* |
| spoon | **žlica** | *zhlih·tsah* |

### ESSENTIAL

| | |
|---|---|
| The wine list/drink menu, please. | **Vinsku kartu/Kartu pića, molim Vas.** *veen·skoo kahr·too/kahr·too pih·chah moh·lihm vahs* |
| What do you recommend? | **Što preporučate?** *shtoh preh·poh·roo·chah·teh* |
| I'd like a bottle/glass of red/white wine. | **Htio** *m***/Htjela** *f* **bih bocu/čašu crnog/ bijelog vina.** *htih·oh/htyeh·lah bih boh·tsoo/ chah·shoo cr·nohg/bih·yeh·lohg veeh·nah* |
| The house wine, please. | **Vino kuće, molim Vas.** *vee·noh koo·cheh moh·lihm vahs* |
| Another bottle/ glass, please. | **Još jednu bocu/čašu, molim Vas.** *yohsh yeh·dnoo boh·tsoo/chah·shoo moh·lihm vahs* |
| I'd like a local beer. | **Htio** *m***/Htjela** *f* **bih lokalno pivo.** *htih·oh/htyeh·lah bih loh·kahl·noh pih·voh* |
| Can I buy you a drink? | **Mogu li Vas počastiti pićem?** *moh·goo lih vahs poh·chah·stih·tih pih·chehm* |
| Cheers! | **Živjeli!** *zhih·vyeh·lih* |
| A coffee/tea, please. | **Kavu/Čaj, molim Vas.** *kah·voo/chahy moh·lihm vahs* |
| With... | **Sa...** *sah...* |
| milk | **mlijekom** *mlih·yeh·kohm* |
| sugar | **šećerom** *sheh·cheh·rohm* |
| artificial sweetener | **umjetnim sladilom** *oo·myeh·tnihm slah·dih·lohm* |
| ...,  please. | **..., molim Vas.** *...moh·lihm vahs* |
| Juice | **Sok** *sohk* |
| Soda | **Gazirani sok** *gah·zih·rah·nih sohk* |
| (Sparkling/Still) Water | **(Mineralnu/Običnu) Vodu** *(mih·neh·rahl·noo/oh·bih·chnoo) voh·doo* |
| Is the water safe to drink? | **Je li voda pitka?** *lih voh·dah pih·tkah* |

## Non-alcoholic Drinks

| | |
|---|---|
| **(ledeni) čaj** *(leh·deh·nih) chahy* | (iced) tea |
| **gazirani sok** *gah·zih·rah·nih sohk* | soda |
| **kava** *kah·vah* | coffee |
| **limunada** *lih·moo·nah·dah* | lemonade |
| **mlijeko** *mlih·yeh·koh* | milk |
| **oranžada** *oh·rahn·zhah·dah* | orangeade |
| **sok** *sohk* | juice |
| **vruća čokolada** | hot chocolate |
| *vroo·chah choh·koh·lah·dah* | |
| **(mineralna/obična) voda** | (sparkling/still) water |
| *(mih·neh·rahl·nah/oh·bih·chnah) voh·dah* | |

The most popular non-alcoholic drink is **kava** (coffee) and going out for a coffee has long been a Croatian social tradition. In bars and restaurants, Italian-style espresso is also available, as are cappuccino and café au lait. Macchiato, coffee with a drop of milk, is popular especially in Dalmatia. **Turska kava** (Turkish coffee), which is very strong, is also available.

## YOU MAY HEAR...

**Želite li nešto piti?** *zheh·lih·teh lih neh·shto pih·tih* Can I get you a drink?

**S mlijekom ili šećerom?** With milk or sugar?
*s mlih·yeh·kohm ih·lih sheh·cheh·rohm*

**Mineralnu ili običnu vodu?** Sparkling or still water?
*mih·neh·rahl·noo ih·lih oh·bih·chnoo voh·doo*

## Aperitifs, Cocktails & Liqueurs

| | |
|---|---|
| **džin** *jihn* | gin |
| **konjak** *koh·nyahk* | scotch |
| **liker Maraskino** *lih·kehr mah·rah·skih·noh* | maraschino liqueur |
| **loza** *loh·zah* | grape brandy |
| **prošek** *proh·shehk* | sweet wine |
| **rakija** *rah·kih·yah* | brandy |
| **rum** *room* | rum |
| **tekila** *teh·kih·lah* | tequila |
| **travarica** *trah·vah·rih·tsah* | herbal brandy |
| **viski** *vih·skih* | whisky |
| **votka** *voht·kah* | vodka |

Croatia is well-known for its aperitifs, such as **domaće rakije** (domestic brandies); **loza**, a Croatian grappa; and **travarica**, an herb-flavored brandy. **Prošek**, a very sweet wine, can be served as an aperitif or after-dinner drink. **Maraschino** is the well-known liqueur from Zadar; it is distilled from the Dalmatian marasca cherry and prepared according to a traditional recipe created by pharmacists of the Dominican monastery at the beginning of 16th century.

## Beer

| | | |
|---|---|---|
| **bezalkoholno** *beh-zahl-koh-hohl-noh* | | non-alcoholic |
| **lager/pilsner** *lah-gehr/pihl-snehr* | | lager/pilsner |
| **lokalno/uvozno** *loh-kahl-noh/oo-voh-znoh* | | local/imported |
| **pivo** *pih-voh* | | beer |

The most popular Croatian brands of beer include **Karlovačko™** and **Ožujsko™**. These are light pilsner-type drinks. Other Croatian brands available are: **Pan™**, **Osiječko™**, **Tomislav™** and **Rally™** (non-alcoholic).

**pola litra** *poh·lah lih·trah* — pint
**tamno/svijetlo** *tah·mnoh/svih·yeh·tloh* — dark/light
**u boci/točeno** *oo boh·tsih/toh·cheh·noh* — bottled/draft

## Wine

**crno/bijelo** *cr·noh/bih·yeh·loh* — red/white
**desertno vino** *deh·sehr·tnoh vee·noh* — dessert wine
**kuće/stolno** *koo·cheh/stohl·noh* — house/table
**pjenušavo** *pyeh·noo·shah·voh* — sparkling
**suho/slatko** *soo·hoh/slah·tkoh* — dry/sweet
**šampanjac** *shahm·pah·nyahts* — champagne
**vino** *vee·noh* — wine

Pelješac is the most famous wine region in Croatia, and 80% of production is red wine. **Dingač** is the most widely available Croatian red wine; it has an alcohol content of about 15%. Also popular are: **viško, hvarsko, kaštelansko** and wine from Istria. Istrian Malvazija is the country's most famous white grape variety.

# On the Menu

| | |
|---|---|
| **ajvar** *ahy·vahr* | red pepper relish |
| **ananas** *ah·nah·nahs* | pineapple |
| **anis** *ah·nihs* | fennel |
| **aperitiv** *ah·peh·rih·tihv* | aperitif |
| **artičok** *ahr·tih·chohk* | artichoke |
| **avokado** *ah·voh·kah·doh* | avocado |
| **badem** *bah·dehm* | almond |
| **bakalar** *bah·kah·lahr* | cod |
| **bakalar** *bah·kah·lahr* | haddock |
| **bamija** *bah·mih·yah* | okra |
| **banana** *bah·nah·nah* | banana |
| **bedro** *beh·droh* | loin |
| **bijeli mekani** *bih·yeh·lih meh·kah·nih sihr* | cottage cheese |
| **biljka** *beely·kah* | herb |
| **bjelance** *byeh·lahn·tseh* | egg yolk |
| **blitva** *bliht·vah* | Swiss chard |
| **bomboni** *bohm·boh·nih* | candy [sweets] |
| **bomboni** *bohm·boh·nih* | sweets |
| **borovnica** *boh·rohv·nih·tsah* | blueberry |
| **bosiljak** *boh·sih·lyahk* | basil |
| **breskva** *brehs·kvah* | peach |
| **brusnica** *broo·snih·tsah* | cranberry |
| **bubreg** *boo·brehg* | kidney |
| **bujon** *boo·yohn* | consommé |
| **celer** *tseh·lehr* | celery |
| **cikorija** *tsih·koh·rih·yah* | chicory |
| **cikorija** *tsih·koh·rih·yah* | escarole [chicory] |
| **cimet** *tsih·meht* | cinnamon |
| **cipal** *tsih·pahl* | red mullet |

| | |
|---|---|
| **crni ribiz** *tsr·nih rih·bihz* | black currant |
| **crveni kupus** *cr·veh·nih koo·poos* | red cabbage |
| **crveni ribiz** *cr·veh·nih rih·bihz* | red currant |
| **čaj** *chahy* | tea |
| **češnjak** *cheh·shnyahk* | garlic |
| **čevapčići** *cheh·vahp·chih·chih* | rolls of ground meat, grilled |
| **čips** *chihps* | potato chips [crisps] |
| **čokolada** *choh·koh·lah·dah* | chocolate |
| **dagnja** *dah·gnyah* | mussels |
| **datulje** *dah·too·lyeh* | dates |
| **desertno vino** *deh·sehr·tnoo vee·noh* | dessert wine |
| **dinja** *dih·nyah* | melon |
| **divljač** *dihv·lyahch* | game |
| **divljač** *dihv·lyahch* | venison |
| **džin** *jihn* | gin |
| **đumbir** *joom·bihr* | ginger |
| **endivija** *ehn·dih·vih·yah* | endive |
| **fritule** *frih·too·leh* | fritter |
| **gazirani sok** *gah·zih·rah·nih sohk* | soda |
| **gljiva** *glyih·vah* | mushroom |
| **gljiva gomoljika** *glyih·vah goh·moh·lyih·kah* | truffles |

| | |
|---|---|
| **goljenica** *goh·lyeh·nih·tsah* | shank |
| **govedina** *goh·veh·dih·nah* | beef |
| **goveđi bubrežnjak** *goh·veh·jih boo·breh·zhnyahk* | sirloin |
| **grah** *grahh* | bean |
| **grahova klica** *grah·hoh·vah klih·tsah* | bean sprouts |
| **grašak** *grah·shahk* | peas |
| **grejpfrut** *grehyp·froot* | grapefruit |
| **grgeč** *grgehch* | bass |
| **grgeč** *grgehch* | sea perch |
| **grožđica** *grohzh·dih·tsah* | raisin |
| **grožđe** *grohzh·jeh* | grapes |
| **guska** *goo·skah* | goose |
| **hamburger** *hahm·boor·gehr* | hamburger |
| **haringa** *hah·rihn·gah* | herring |
| **hladni naresci** *hlah·dnih nah·rehs·tsih* | cold cuts [charcuterie] |
| **hobotnica** *hoh·boh·tnih·tsah* | octopus |
| **inćun** *ihn·choon* | anchovy |
| **indijski oraščić** *ihn·dihy·skih oh·rahsh·chihch* | cashew |
| **iverak** *ih·veh·rahk* | halibut |

| | |
|---|---|
| **iznutrice** *ihz·noo·trih·tseh* | organ meat [offal] |
| **jabuka** *yah·boo·kah* | apple |
| **jabukovača** *yah·boo·koh·vah·chah* | cider |
| **jagoda** *yah·goh·dah* | strawberry |
| **jaje** *yah·yeh* | egg |
| **jakovska kapica** *yah·kohv·skah kah·pih·tsah* | scallop |
| **janje y**ah·nyeh | lamb |
| **jastog** *yah·stohg* | lobster |
| **jegulja** *yeh·goo·lyah* | eel |
| **jetrica** *yeh·trih·tsah* | liver |
| **jezik** *yeh·zihk* | tongue |
| **jogurt** *yoh·goort* | yogurt |
| **juha** *yoo·hah* | soup |
| **juha od mesa** *yoo·hah ohd meh·sah* | broth |
| **kadulja** *kah·doo·lyah* | sage |
| **kamenica** *kah·meh·nih·tsah* | oyster |
| **kapar** *kah·pahr* | caper |
| **karamel** *kah·rah·mehl* | caramel |
| **karfiol** *kahr·fih·ohl* | cauliflower |
| **kava** *kah·vah* | coffee |

| | |
|---|---|
| **kečap** *keh·chahp* | ketchup |
| **kesten** *keh·stehn* | chestnut |
| **kikiriki** *kih·kih·rih·kih* | peanut |
| **kim** *kihm* | cumin |
| **kiseli krastavci** *kih·seh·lih krah·stahv·tsih* | gherkin |
| **kiseli krastavci** *kih·seh·lih krah·stahv·tsih* | pickle |
| **kiselo vrhnje** *kih·seh·loh vrh·nyeh* | sour cream |
| **kivi** *kih·vih* | kiwi |
| **klinčić** *klihn·chihch* | clove |
| **kobasica** *koh·bah·sih·tsah* | sausage |
| **kokos** *koh·kohs* | coconut |
| **kolač** *koh·lahch* | cake |
| **kolači** *koh·lah·chih* | pastry |
| **kolačić** *koh·lah·chihch* | cookie [biscuit] |
| **koljenica** *koh·lyeh·nih·tsah* | leg |
| **kompot** *kohm·poht* | stewed fruit |
| **konjak** *koh·nyahk* | scotch |
| **kopar** *koh·pahr* | dill |

| | |
|---|---|
| **korijander** *koh·rih·yahn·dehr* | cilantro [coriander] |
| **kotlet** *koht·leht* | chop |
| **koza** *koh·zah* | goat |
| **kozice** *koh·zih·tseh* | shrimp |
| **kozji sir** *koh·zyih sihr* | goat cheese |
| **krastavac** *krah·stah·vahts* | cucumber |
| **krasuljica** *krah·soo·lyih·tsah* | chervil |
| **kreker** *kreh·kehr* | cracker |
| **kruh** *krooh* | bread |
| **krumpir** *kroom·pihr* | potato |
| **kruška** *kroo·shkah* | pear |
| **krvavica** *kr·vah·vih·tsah* | blood sausage |
| **kulen** *koo·lehn* | sausage, spicy, flavored with paprika (Slavonia) |
| **kumin** *koo·mihn* | caraway |
| **kunić** *koo·nihch* | rabbit |
| **kupina** *koo·pih·nah* | blackberry, raspberry |
| **kupus** *koo·poos* | cabbage |
| **leća** *leh·chah* | lentil |
| **led** *lehd* | ice |
| **liganj** *lih·gahny* | squid |

**liker** *lih·kehr*                         liqueur
**liker od naranče**                    orange liqueur
*lih·kehr ohd nah·rahn·cheh*
**limeta** *lih·meh·tah*              lime
**limun** *lih·moon*                     lemon
**limunada**                                lemonade
**list** *lihst*                                 sole
**losos** *loh·sohs*                      salmon
**lovorov list** *loh·voh·rohv lihst*   bay leaf
**lubenica** *loo·beh·nih·tsah*   watermelon
**lubin** *loo·bihn*                      sea bass
**luk** *look*                                 onion
**lješnjak** *lyeh·shnyahk*        hazelnut
**ljuta papričica**                     chili pepper
*lyoo·tah pah·prih·chi·tsah*
**ljuti umak** *lyoo·tih oo·mahk*   hot pepper sauce
**mahune** *mah·hoo·neh*        green bean
**majčina dušica**                     thyme
*mahy·chih·nah doo·shih·tsah*
**majoneza** *mah·yoh·neh·zah*   mayonnaise
**makaroni** *mah·kah·roh·nih*   macaroni

| | |
|---|---|
| **makovnjača** *mah·kohv·nyah·chah* | poppy seed roll |
| **mandarina** *mahn·dah·rih·nah* | tangerine |
| **mango** *mahn·goo* | mango |
| **marcipan** *mahr·tsih·pahn* | marzipan |
| **marelica** *mah·reh·lih·tsah* | apricot |
| **margarin** *mahr·gah·rihn* | margarine |
| **marmelada** *mahr·meh·lah·dah* | marmalade |
| **maslac** *mah·slahts* | butter |
| **maslina** *mah·slih·nah* | olive |
| **maslinovo ulje** *mah·slih·noh·voh oo·lyeh* | olive oil |
| **med** *mehd* | honey |
| **meso** *meh·soh* | meat |
| **meso od rakova** *meh·soh ohd rah·koh·vah* | crabmeat |
| **metvica** *meh·tvih·tsah* | mint |
| **milk shake** *mihlk·shehyk* | milk shake |
| **milnci** *mlihn·tsih* | pasta, thinly rolled |
| **mladi luk** *mlah·dih look* | scallion [spring onion] |
| **mlijeko** *mlih·yeh·koh* | milk |

| | |
|---|---|
| **mljeveno meso** | chopped meat |
| *mlyeh·veh·noh meh·soh* | |
| **morski plodovi** | seafood |
| *mohr·skih ploh·doh·vih* | |
| **mrkva** *mr·kvah* | carrot |
| **muškatov orah** | nutmeg |
| *moo·shkah·tohv oh·rahh* | |
| **nar** *nahr* | pomegranate |
| **naranča** *nah·rahn·chah* | orange |
| **nugat** *noo·gaht* | nougat |
| **ocat** *oh·tsaht* | vinegar |
| **odojak** *oh·doh·yahk* | suckling pig |
| **odrezak** *oh·dreh·zahk* | steak |
| **ogrozd** *oh·grohzd* | gooseberry |
| **omlet** *ohm·leht* | omelet |
| **orah** *oh·rahh* | walnut |
| **orahnjača** *oh·rahh·nyah·chah* | walnut roll |
| **orasi** *oh·rah·sih* | nuts |
| **origano** *oh·rih·gah·noh* | oregano |
| **oslić** *oh·slihch* | hake |
| **ovca** *ohv·tsah* | mutton |

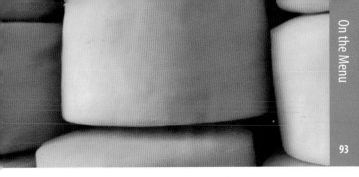

**palačinka** *pah·lah·chihn·kah* — pancake
**papar** *pah·pahr* — pepper (seasoning)
**paprika** *pah·prih·kah* — paprika, pepper (vegetable)
**pastrva** *pah·str·vah* — trout
**paški sir** *pahsh·kih sihr* — Pag cheese (hard, sheep's cheese from the island of Pag)

**pašteta** *pah·shteh·tah* — pâté
**pašticada** *pah·shtih·tsah·dah* — stewed beef with proscuitto, marinated in lemon, wine and rosemary

**patka** *pah·tkah* — duck
**patlidžan** *pah·tlih·jahn* — eggplant [aubergine]
**pečena govedina** *peh·cheh·nah goh·veh·dih·nah* — roast beef

**pečenje** *peh·cheh·nyeh* — roast
**pekmez** *pehk·mehz* — jam
**perad** *peh·rahd* — poultry
**perlinka** *pehr·lihn·kah* — guinea fowl
**peršin** *pehr·shihn* — parsley
**piletina** *pih·leh·tih·nah* — chicken

| | |
|---|---|
| **pivo** *pih·voh* | beer |
| **pizza** *pih·tsah* | pizza |
| **pleće** *pleh·cheh* | shoulder |
| **pohani** *sir poh·hah·nih sihr* | cheese, fried in breadcrumbs |
| **polenta** *poh·lehn·tah* | cornmeal |
| **pomfrit** *pohm·friht* | French fries |
| **ponutrica** *poh·noo·trih·tsah* | giblet |
| **poriluk** *poh·rih·look* | leek |
| **porto** *pohr·toh* | port |
| **potočarka** *poh·toh·chahr·kah* | watercress |
| **povrće** *poh·vr·cheh* | vegetable |
| **prepelica** *preh·peh·lih·tsah* | quail |
| **prokulice** *proh·koo·lih·tseh* | Brussels sprouts |
| **(pileća) prsa** *(pih·leh·chah) pr·sah* | breast (of chicken) |
| **pršut** *pr·shoot* | smoked ham |
| **pšenica** *psheh·nihl·tsah* | wheat |
| **purica** *poo·rih·tsah* | turkey |
| **puslica** *poo·slih·tsah* | meringue |
| **puž** *poozh* | snail |
| **rabarbara** *rah·bahr·bah·rah* | rhubarb |
| **rajčica** *rahy·chih·tsah* | tomato |

| | |
|---|---|
| **rak** *rahk* | crab |
| **rakija** *rah·kih·yah* | brandy |
| **ražnjići** *rahzh·nyih·chih* | meat kebabs |
| **repa** *reh·pah* | beet |
| **repa** *reh·pah* | turnip |
| **rezanac** *reh·zah·nahts* | noodle |
| **riba** *rih·bah* | fish |
| **riblja pašteta** *rih·blyah pah·shteh·tah* | fish pâté |
| **riža** *rih·zhah* | rice |
| **rižot** *rih·zhoht* | risotto |
| **rolada** *roh·lah·dah* | roll |
| **rotkva** *roht·kvah* | radish |
| **rožata** *roh·zhah·tah* | creme caramel |
| **rum** *room* | rum |
| **ružmarin** *roozh·mah·rihn* | rosemary |
| **sabljarka** *sah·blyahr·kah* | swordfish |
| **salama** *sah·lah·mah* | salami |
| **salata** *sah·lah·tah* | salad |
| **salata od hobotnice** | octopus salad |
| *sah·lah·ta ohd hoh·boh·tnih·tseh* | |
| **sardina** *sahr·dih·nah* | sardine |

| | |
|---|---|
| **savijača** *sah·vih·yah·chah* | strudel |
| **sendvič** *sehn·dvihch* | sandwich |
| **senf** *sehnf* | mustard |
| **sir** *sihr* | cheese |
| **sir sa plijesni** *sihr sah plih·yeh·snih* | blue cheese |
| **skuša** *skoo·shah* | mackerel |
| **sladoled** *slah·doh·lehd* | ice cream |
| **slani inćuni** *slah·nih ihn·choo·nih* | salted anchovies |
| **slanina** *slah·nih·nah* | bacon |
| **slanutak** *slah·noo·tahk* | chick pea |
| **slatki i kiseli umak** *slah·tkih ih kih·seh·lih oo·mahk* | sweet and sour sauce |
| **slatki krumpir** *slah·tkih kroom·pihr* | sweet potato |
| **slatki kukuruz** *slah·tkih koo·koo·rooz* | sweet corn |
| **smokva** *smoh·kvah* | fig |
| **soja** *soh·yah* | soy [soya] |
| **sojin plod** *soh·yihn plohd* | soybean [soya bean] |
| **sojino mlijeko** *soh·yih·noh mlih·yeh·koh* | soymilk [soya milk] |

| | |
|---|---|
| **sok** *sohk* | juice |
| **sol** *sohl* | salt |
| **spirit** *spih·riht* | spirits |
| **srce** *sr·tseh* | heart |
| **suha šljiva** *soo·hah shlyih·vah* | prune |
| **surutka** *soo·roo·tkah* | buttermilk |
| **svinjetina** *svih·nyeh·tih·nah* | pork |
| **svježi sir** *svyeh·zhih sih* | cream cheese |
| **šafran** *shah·frahn* | saffron |
| **šećer** *sheh·chehr* | sugar |
| **šeri** *sheh·rih* | sherry |
| **škalonja** *shkah·loh·nyah* | shallot |
| **školjka** *shkoh·lykah* | clam |
| **školjka** *shkoh·lykah* | shellfish |
| **šljiva** *shlyih·vah* | plum |
| **špageti** *shpah·geh·tih* | spaghetti |
| **šparoga** *shpah·roh·gah* | asparagus |
| **špinat** *shpih·naht* | spinach |
| **šunka** *shoon·kah* | ham |
| **tarkanj** *tahr·kahny* | tarragon |
| **teletina** *teh·leh·tih·nah* | veal |

| | |
|---|---|
| **tikva** *tih·kvah* | pumpkin |
| **tikva** *tih·kvah* | squash |
| **tikvica** *tih·kvih·tsah* | zucchini [courgette] |
| **tofu** *toh·foo* | tofu |
| **tonik** *toh·nihk* | tonic water |
| **torta** *tohr·tah* | pie |
| **tost** *tohst* | toast |
| **trešnja** *treh·shnyah* | cherry |
| **tripice** *trih·pih·tseh* | tripe |
| **tučeno vrhnje** *too·cheh·noh vrh·nyeh* | whipped cream |
| **tuna** *too·nah* | tuna |
| **umak** *oo·mahk* | sauce |
| **umak od češnjaka** *oo·mahk ohd cheh·shnyah·kah* | garlic sauce |
| **umak od soje** *oo·mahk ohd soh·yeh* | soy sauce |
| **umjetno sladilo** *oo·myeh·tnoh slah·dih·loh* | artificial sweetener |
| **uštipak** *oo·shtih·pahk* | doughnut |
| **vafle** *vah·fleh* | waffle |
| **vanilija** *vah·nih·lih·yah* | vanilla |
| **vermut** *vehr·moot* | vermouth |

| | |
|---|---|
| **vino** *vee·noh* | wine |
| **viski** *vih·skih* | whisky |
| **višnja** *vihsh·nyah* | sour cherry |
| **vlasac** *vlah·sahts* | chives |
| **voće** *voh·cheh* | fruit |
| **voda** *voh·dah* | water |
| **vol** *vohl* | ox |
| **volovski rep** *voh·lohv·skih rehp* | oxtail |
| **votka** *voh·tkah* | vodka |
| **vrhnje** *vrh·nyeh* | cream |
| **začini** *zah·chih·nih* | spices |
| **Zagorski kotlet** *zah·gohr·skih koh·tleht* | beef cutlet |
| **Zagrebački odrezak** *zah·greh·bah·chkih oh·dreh·zahk* | veal steak |
| **zakuska** *zah·koo·skah* | snack |
| **zelena salata** *zeh·leh·nah sah·lah·tah* | lettuce |
| **žitarica** *zhih·tah·rih·tsah* | cereal |

# People

## ESSENTIAL

| | | |
|---|---|---|
| Hello! | **Bog!** *bohg* | |
| Hi! | **Zdravo!** *zdrah·voh* | |
| How are you? | **Kako ste?** *kah·koh steh* | *Fala* |
| Fine, thanks. | **Dobro, hvala.** *doh·broh hvah·lah* | |
| Excuse me! | **Oprostite!** *oh·proh·stih·teh* | |
| Do you speak English? | **Govorite li engleski?** | |
| | *goh·voh·rih·teh lih ehn·gleh·skih* | |
| What's your name? | **Kako se zovete?** | |
| | *kah·koh seh zoh·veh·teh* | |
| My name is... | **Moje ime je...** *moh·yeh ih·meh yeh...* | |
| Nice to meet you. | **Drago mi je.** *drah·goh mih yeh* | |
| Where are you from? | **Odakle ste?** *oh·dah·kleh steh* | |
| I'm from the U.S./U.K. | **Ja sam iz S.A.D.-a/Velike Britanije.** | |
| | *yah sahm ihz ehs·ah·deh·ah/veh·lih·keh* | |
| | *brih·tah·nih·yeh* | |
| What do you do? | **Čime se bavite?** | |
| | *chee·meh seh bah·vih·teh* | |
| I work for... | **Radim za...** *rah·dihm zah...* | |
| I'm a student. | **Studiram.** *stoo·dih·rahm* | |
| I'm retired. | **U mirovini sam.** | |
| | *oo mih·roh·vih·nih sahm* | |
| Do you like...? | **Sviđa li Vam se...?** | |
| | *svih·jah lih vahm seh...* | |
| Goodbye. | **Doviđenja.** *doh·vih·jeh·nyah* | |
| See you later. | **Vidimo se kasnije.** | |
| | *vih·dih·moh seh kah·snih·yeh* | |

There are two forms for "you" in Croatian. The informal forms **ti** (singular) or **vi** (plural) are used when talking to friends, relatives and among young people. **Vi** (formal) is used when speaking to one or more persons in a formal setting. The formal **gospodine** (Sir), **gospođo** (Mrs.), **gospođice** (Miss) can be used in the same situations as **Vi**. It is considered impolite to address people you don't know by their first name. For more on Grammar, see page 162.

## Language Difficulties

| | | |
|---|---|---|
| Do you speak English? | **Govorite li engleski?** | goh·voh·rih·teh lih ehn·gleh·skih |
| Does anyone here speak English? | **Da li ovdje itko govori engleski?** | dah lih ohv·dyeh ih·tkoh goh·voh·rih ehn·gleh·skih |
| I don't speak (much) Croatian. | **Ne govorim (mnogo) hrvatski.** | neh goh·voh·rihm (mnoh·goh) hr·vaht·skih |
| Can you speak more slowly? | **Možete li govoriti sporije?** | moh·zheh·teh lih goh·voh·rih·tih spoh·rih·yeh |
| Can you repeat that? | **Možete li to ponoviti?** | moh·zheh·teh lih poh·noh·vih·tih |
| Excuse me? | **Oprostite?** | oh·proh·stih·teh |
| What was that? | **Što je to?** | shtoh yeh toh |
| Can you spell it? | **Možete li sricati to?** | moh·zhe·teh lih srih·tsah·tih toh |
| Please write it down. | **Molim Vas napišite.** | moh·lihm vahs nah·pih·shih·teh |
| Can you translate this into English for me? | **Možete li mi to prevesti na engleski?** | moh·zheh·teh lih mih toh preh·veh·stih ne ehn·gleh·skih |
| What does this/ that mean? | **Što ovo/to znači?** | shtoh oh·voh/toh znah·chih |
| I understand. | **Razumijem.** | rah·zoo·mih·yehm |
| I don't understand. | **Ne razumijem.** | neh rah·zoo·mih·yehm |
| Do you understand? | **Razumijete li?** | rah·zoo·mih·yeh·teh lih |

## YOU MAY HEAR...

**Malo govorim engleski.**
*mah·loh goh·voh·rihm ehn·gleh·skih*

**Ne govorim engleski.**
*neh goh·voh·rihm ehn·gleh·skih*

I only speak a little English.

I don't speak English.

## Making Friends

| | |
|---|---|
| Hello./Hi! | **Bog!** *bohg* |
| Good morning. | **Dobro jutro.** *doh·broh yoo·troh* |
| Good day. | **Dobar dan.** *doh·bahr dahn* |
| Good evening. | **Dobra večer.** *doh·brah veh·chehr* |
| My name is... | **Moje ime je...** *moh·yeh ih·meh yeh...* |
| What's your name? | **Kako se zovete?** *kah·koh seh zoh·veh·teh* |
| I'd like to introduce you to... | **Htio** *m*/**Htjela** *f* **bih Vas upoznati sa...** *htih·oh/htyeh·lah bih vahs oo·pohz·nah·tih sa...* |
| Pleased to meet you. | **Drago mi je.** *drah·goh mih yeh* |
| How are you? | **Kako ste?** *kah·koh steh* |
| Fine, thanks. And you? | **Dobro, hvala. A vi?** *doh·broh hvah·lah. Ah vee* |

To greet someone in Croatian, you can say **bog** (hello), **dobro jutro** (good morning) or **dobar dan** (good day). When leaving, say **doviđenja** (goodbye). Close acquaintances usually kiss on each cheek, otherwise, a handshake is the norm. Always remember to address someone you do not know using the **Vi** (polite/plural) form for "you".

## Travel Talk

| | | |
|---|---|---|
| I'm here... | **Ovdje sam...** | *ohv·dyeh sahm...* |
| on business | **poslovno** | *poh·sloh·vnoh* |
| on vacation [holiday] | **na odmoru** | *nah ohd·moh·roo* |
| studying | **na studijima** | *nah stoo·dih·yih·mah* |
| I'm staying for... | **Ostajem...** | *oh·stah·yehm...* |
| I've been here... | **Ovdje sam...** | *ohv·dyeh sahm...* |
| a day | **jedan dan** | *yeh·dahn dahn* |
| a week | **tjedan dana** | *tyeh·dahn dah·nah* |
| a month | **mjesec dana** | *myeh·sehts dah·nah* |
| Where are you from? | **Odakle ste?** | *oh·dah·kleh steh* |
| I'm from... | **Ja sam iz...** | *jah sahm ihz...* |

For Numbers, see page 169.

## Personal

| | | |
|---|---|---|
| Who are you with? | **S kim ste ovdje?** *skeem steh ohv·dyeh* | |
| I'm here alone. | **Ovjde sam sam** *m*/**sama** *f*. | |
| | *ohv·dyeh sahm sahm/sah·mah* | |
| I'm with my... | **Sa...sam.** *sah...sahm* | |
| husband/wife | **suprugom** *soo·proo·gohm* | |
| boyfriend/girlfriend | **dečkom/djevojkom** *dehch·kohm/dyeh·vohy·kohm* | |
| brother/sister | **bratom/sestrom** *brah·tohm/seh·strohm* | |
| mother/father | **majkom/ocem** *mahy·kohm/oh·tsehm* | |
| colleague/friend | **kolegom/prijateljem** *koh·leh·gohm/prih·yah·teh·lyehm* | |
| When's your birthday? | **Kada Vam je rođendan?** *kah·dah vahm yeh* | |
| | *roh·jehn·dahn* | |
| How old are you? | **Koliko Vam je godina?** | |
| | *koh·lih·koh vahm yeh goh·dih·nah* | |
| I'm... | **...mi je godina.** *...mih yeh goh·dih·nah* | |
| Are you married? | **Jeste li oženjen** *m*/**udana** *f*? | |
| | *yeh·steh lih oh·zheh·nyehn/oo·dah·nah* | |
| I'm... | **Ja sam...** *jah sahm...* | |
| single | **neoženjen** *m*/**neudana** *f* | |
| | *neh·oh·zheh·nyehn/neh·oo·dah·nah* | |
| in a relationship | **u vezi** *oo veh·zih* | |
| engaged | **zaručen** *m*/**zaručena** *f* *zah·roo·chehn/zah·roo·cheh·nah* | |
| married | **oženjen** *m*/**udana** *f* *oh·zheh·nyehn/oo·dah·nah* | |
| divorced | **razveden** *m*/**razvedena** *f* | |
| | *rah·zveh·dehn/rah·zveh·deh·nah* | |
| separated | **razdvojen** *m*/**razdvojena** *f* | |
| | *rahz·dvoh·yehn/rahz·dvoh·yeh·nah* | |
| widowed | **udovac** *m*/**udovica** *f* *oo·doh·vahts/oo·doh·vih·tsah* | |
| Do you have children/ | **Imate li djece/unuke?** | |
| grandchildren? | *ih·mah·teh lih dyeh·tseh/oo·noo·keh* | |

## Work & School

| | |
|---|---|
| What do you do for a living? | **Čime se bavite?** *chee·meh seh bah·vih·teh* |
| What are you studying? | **Što studirate?** *shtoh stoo·dih·rah·teh* |
| I'm studying... | **Studiram hrvatski.** *stoo·dih·rahm hr·vaht·skih* |
| I... | **Ja...** *ja...* |
|    work full-time/ part-time | **radim puno radno vrijeme/honorarno** *rah·dihm poo·noh rah·dnoh vrih·yeh·meh/hoh·noh·rahr·noh* |
|    do freelance work | **radim samostalno** *rah·dihm sah·moh·stahl·noh* |
|    am a consultant | **sam savjetnik** *sahm sah·vyeh·tnihk* |
|    self-employed | **samozaposlen** *sah·moh·zah·poh·slehn* |
|    am unemployed | **sam nezaposlen** *sahm neh·zah·poh·slehn* |
|    work at home | **radim doma** *rah·dihm doh·mah* |
|    retired | **umirovljenik...** *oo·mih·roh·vlyeh·nee·kh* |
| Who do you work for? | **Za koga radite?** *zah koh·gah rah·dih·teh* |
| I work for... | **Radim za...** *rah·dihm zah...* |
| Here's my business card. | **Izvolite moju vizit karticu.** *ihz·voh·lih·teh moh·yoo vih·ziht kahr·tih·tsoo* |

For Business Travel, see page 141.

## Weather

| | |
|---|---|
| What's the forecast? | **Kakva je vremenska prognoza?** *kah·kvah yeh vreh·mehn·skah proh·gnoh·zah* |
| What beautiful/ terrible weather! | **Koje predivno/grozno vrijeme!** *koh·yeh preh·dih·vnoh/groh·znoh vrih·yeh·meh* |
| It's... | **...je.** *...yeh* |
|    cool/warm | **Svježe/Toplo** *svyeh·zheh/toh·ploh* |
|    cold/hot | **Hladno/Vruće** *hlah·dnoh/vroo·cheh* |
|    rainy/sunny | **Kiša/Sunčano** *kih·shah/soon·chah·noh* |
|    snowy/icy | **Snježno/Mraz** *snyeh·zhnoh/mrahz* |
| Do I need a jacket/ an umbrella? | **Treba li mi jakna/kišobran?** *treh·bah lih mih yah·knah/kih·shoh·brahn* |

## Romance

### ESSENTIAL

| | |
|---|---|
| Would you like to go out for a drink/dinner? | **Želite li izaći na piće/večeru?** zheh·lih·te lih ih·zah·chih nah pih·cheh/veh·cheh·roo |
| What are your for tonight/tomorrow? | **Mogu li dobiti Vaš broj?** moh·goo lih doh·bih·tih vahsh brohy |
| Can I have your number? | **Mogu li dobiti Vaš broj?** moh·goo lih doh·bih·tih vahsh brohy |
| Can I join you? | **Mogu li Vam se pridružiti?** moh·goo lih vahm seh prih·droo·zhih·tih |
| Can I get you a drink? | **Mogu li Vas počastiti pićem?** moh·goo lih vahs poh·chah·stih·tih pih·chehm |
| I like you. | **Sviđaš mi se.** svih·jahsh mih seh |
| I love you. | **Volim te.** voh·lihm teh |

### The Dating Game

| | |
|---|---|
| Would you like to go out for…? | **Želite li izaći na…?** zheh·lih·teh lih ih·zah·chih nah… |
| coffee | **kavu** kah·voo |
| a drink | **piće** pih·cheh |
| dinner | **večeru** veh·cheh·roo |
| What are your plans for…? | **Kakvi su Vam planovi za…?** kah·kvih soo vahm plah·noh·vih zah… |
| today | **danas** dah·nahs |
| tonight | **večeras** veh·cheh·rah |
| tomorrow | **sutra** soo·trah |
| this weekend | **ovaj vikend** oh·vahy vih·kehnd |
| Where would you like to go? | **Gdje želite ići?** gdyeh zheh·lih·teh ih·chih |

| | |
|---|---|
| I'd like to go to… | **Htio m/Htjela f bih ići…** |
| | *htih·oh/htyeh·lah bih ih·chih…* |
| Do you like…? | **Sviđa li Vam se…?** *svih·jah lih vahm seh…* |
| Can I have your number/email? | **Mogu li dobiti Vaš broj/e-mail?** |
| | *moh·goo lih doh·bih·tih vahsh brohy/ee·mehyl* |
| Are you on Facebook/Twitter? | **Jesi li na Facebooku/Twitteru?** |
| | *yeh·sih lih nah fehys·boo·koo/twih·teh·roo* |
| Can I join you? | **Mogu li Vam se pridružiti?** |
| | *moh·goo lih vahm seh prih·droo·zhih·tih* |
| You're very attractive. | **Vrlo ste privlačni.** *vrloh steh prih·vlah·chnih* |
| Let's go somewhere quieter. | **Idemo na neko mirnije mjesto.** |
| | *ih·deh·moh nah neh·koh mihr·nih·yeh myeh·stoh* |

For Communications, see page 49.

## Accepting & Rejecting

| | |
|---|---|
| I'd love to. | **Rado.** *rah·doh* |
| Where should we meet? | **Gdje ćemo se sastati?** |
| | *gdyeh cheh·moh seh sah·stah·tih* |
| I'll meet you at the bar/your hotel. | **Naći ćemo se u baru/vašim hotelu.** *nah·chih* |
| | *cheh·moh seh oo bah·roo/vah·shihm hoh·teh·loo* |
| I'll come by at… | **Doći ću u…** *doh·chih choo oo…* |

| I'm busy. | **Zauzet m/Zauzeta f sam.** |
| | *zah·oo·zeht/zah·oo·zeh·tah sahm* |
| I'm not interested. | **Ne zanima me.** *neh zah·nih·mah meh* |
| Leave me alone. | **Ostavite me na miru.** *oh·stah·vih·teh meh nah mih·roo* |
| Stop bothering me! | **Prestanite mi dosađivati!** |
| | *preh·stah·nih·teh mih doh·sah·jih·vah·tih* |

For Time, see page 170.

## Getting Intimate

| Can I hug/kiss you? | **Mogu li Vas zagrliti/poljubiti?** |
| | *moh·goo lih vahs zah·gr·lih·tih/poh·lyoo·bih·tih* |
| Yes. | **Da.** *dah* |
| No. | **Ne.** *neh* |
| Stop! | **Prestanite!** *preh·stah·nih·teh* |
| I like you. | **Sviđaš mi se.** *svih·jahsh mih seh* |
| I love you. | **Volim te.** *voh·lihm teh* |

## Sexual Preferences

| Are you gay? | **Jesi li gay?** *yeh·sih lih gehy* |
| I'm... | **Ja sam...** *jah sahm...* |
|    heterosexual | **heteroseksualac m/heteroseksualka f** |
| | *heh·teh·roh·sehk·soo·ah·lahts/* |
| | *heh·teh·roh·sehk·soo·ahl·kah* |
|    homosexual | **homoseksualac m/homoseksualka f** |
| | *hoh·moh·sehk·soo·ah·lahts/hoh·moh·sehk·soo·ahl·kah* |
|    bisexual | **biseksualac m/biseksualka f** |
| | *bih·sehk·soo·ah·lahhts/bih·sehk·soo·ahl·kah* |
| Do you like men/ women? | **Sviđaju li ti se muškarci/žene?** |
| | *svih·jah·yoo lih tih seh moo·shkahr·tsih/zheh·neh* |
| Let's go to a gay bar/club. | **Idemo u gay bar/klub.** |
| | *ih·deh·moh oo gay bahr/kloob* |

# Leisure Time

## ESSENTIAL

| | |
|---|---|
| Where's the tourist information office? | **Gdje je turistički informativni ured?** *gdyeh yeh too·rih·stih·chkih ihn·fohr·mah·tih·vnih oo·rehd* |
| What are the main attractions? | **Koje su glavne znamenitosti?** *koh·yeh soo glah·vneh znah·meh·nih·toh·stih* |
| Do you have tours in English? | **Imate li ture na engleskom?** *ih·mah·teh lih too·reh nah ehn·gleh·skohm* |
| Can I have a map/ guide? | **Mogu li dobiti zemljopisnu kartu/vodič?** *moh·goo lih doh·bih·tih zeh·mlyoh·pih·snoo kahr·too/voh·dihch* |

## Tourist Information

| | |
|---|---|
| Do you have any | **Imete li informacije na…?** *ih·mah·teh lih ihn·fohr·mah·tsih·yeh nah…* |
| Can you recommend…? | **Možete li preporučiti…?** *moh·zheh·teh· lih preh·poh·roo·chih·tih…* |
| a boat trip | **izlet brodom** *ihz·leht broh·dohm* |
| a bus tour | **turu autobusom** *too·roo ah·oo·toh·boo·sohm* |
| an excursion to… | **izlet u…** *ihz·leht oo* |
| a sightseeing tour | **obilazak znamenitosti** *oh·bih·lah·zahk znah·meh·nih·toh·stih* |

**Turistički informativni ured** (tourist information offices) can provide accommodation tips and reservations, maps, excursion options, information on car or boat rental and money exchange. They are usually located in town centers, at ports and near bus stations. Along the Adriatic coastline, many resorts have their own **informacije** (information offices) or **turističke zajednice** (tourist associations).

## On Tour

| | |
|---|---|
| I'd like to go on the excursion to… | **Htio m/Htjela f bih ići na izlet u…** *htih·oh/htyeh·lah bih ih·chih nah ihz·leht oo…* |
| When's the next tour? | **Kada je sljedeći izlet?** *kah·dah yeh slyeh·deh·chih ihz·leht* |
| Are there tours in English? | **Ima li izleta na engleskom?** *ih·mah lih ihz·leh·tah nah ehn·gleh·skohm* |
| Is there an English guide book/audio guide? | **Ima li vodič na engleskom jeziku/audio vodič?** *ih·mah lih voh·dihch nah ehn·gleh·skohm yeh·zih·koo/ ah·oo·dih·oh voh·dihch* |
| What time do we leave/return? | **Kada krećemo/Kad se vraćamo?** *kah·dah kreh·che·moh/kahd seh vrah·cha·moh* |
| I'd like to see… | **Htio m/Htjela f bih vidjeti…** *htih·oh/htyeh·lah bih vih·dyeh·tih…* |
| Can we stop here…? | **Možemo li se ovdje zaustaviti kako bismo…?** *moh·zheh·moh lih seh ohv·dyeh zah·oo·stah·vih·tih kah·koh bih·smoh…* |
| to take photos | **fotografirali** *foh·toh·grah·fih·rah·lih* |
| for souvenirs | **kupili suvenire** *koo·pih·lih soo·veh·nee·reh* |
| for the toilets | **otišli u zahod** *oh·tih·shlih oo zah·hohd* |
| Can we look around? | **Možemo li razgledati?** *moh·zheh·moh lih rahz·gleh·dah·tih* |
| Is it handicapped-[disabled-] accessible? | **Je li pristupačno za hendikepirane osobe?** *yeh lih prih·stoo·pah·chnoh zah hehn·dih·keh·pih·rah·neh oh·soh·beh* |

For Tickets, see page 19.

## Seeing the Sights

| | |
|---|---|
| Where's…? | **Gdje je…?** *gdyeh yeh…* |
| the battleground | **borilište** *boh·rih·lih·shteh* |

| | | |
|---|---|---|
| the botanical garden | **botanički vrt** | boh·tah·nih·chkih vrt |
| the castle | **dvorac** | dvoh·rahts |
| the downtown area | **centar grada** | tsehn·tahr grah·dah |
| the fountain | **vodoskok** | voh·doh·skohk |
| the library | **knjižnica** | knyih·zhnih·tsah |
| the market | **tržnica** | tr·zhnih·tsah |
| the (war) memorial | **(ratni) spomenik** | (rah·tnih) spoh·meh·nihk |
| the museum | **muzej** | moo·zehy |
| the old town | **stari grad** | stah·rih grahd |
| the park | **park** | pahrk |
| the shopping area | **trgovačka** zona | tr·goh·vah·chkah zoh·nah |
| the theater | **kazalište** | kah·zah·lih·shteh |
| the town square | **gradski trg** | grahd·skih trg |
| Can you show me on the map? | **Možete li mi pokazati na karti?** | moh·zheh·teh lih mih poh·kah·zah·tih nah kahr·tih |
| It's… | **…je** | …yeh |
| amazing | **Divno** | dih·vnoh |
| beautiful | **Prekrasno** | preh·krah·snoh |

Croatia offers many sights for tourists, including majestic old cities, beautiful landscapes and Adriatic coastlines. Among the highlights are: Zagreb, Croatia's capital, is a charming old-world city. **Gornji Grad** (upper town) is the central part of Zagreb, and includes many of the main sights. Dubrovnik, founded in the 7th century and included on the UNESCO World Heritage List, is famed for its old walled town, which has remained intact for centuries. Split is famous for Diocletian's palace, built in the 4th century. Pula is noted for its well-preserved Roman ruins: the temple of the Emperor Augustus and the Arena, an amphitheater built during the 1st and 3rd centuries.

| boring | **Dosadno** *doh·sah·dnoh* |
| interesting | **Zanimljivo** *zah·nih·mlyih·voh* |
| magnificent | **Predivno** *preh·dih·vno* |
| romantic | **Romantično** *roh·mahn·tih·chnoh* |
| strange | **Čudno** *choo·dnoh* |
| stunning | **Veličanstveno** *veh·lih·chahn·stveh·noh* |
| terrible | **Grozno** *groh·znoh* |
| ugly | **Ružno** *roo·zhnoh* |
| I (don't) like it. | **(Ne) Sviđa mi se.** *(neh) svih·jah mih seh* |

For Asking Directions, see page 34.

## Religious Sites

| Where's the…? | **Gdje je…?** *gdyeh yeh…* |
| Catholic/ | **katolička/protestantska** |
| Protestant | *kah·toh·lih·chkah/proh·teh·stahnt·skah* |
| church | **crkva** *tsr·kvah* |
| mosque | **džamija** *jah·mih·yah* |
| shrine | **svetište** *sveh·tih·shteh* |
| synagogue | **sinagoga** *sih·nah·goh·gah* |
| What time is mass/ | **U koliko sati je misa/služba?** |
| the service? | *oo koh·lih·koh sah·tih yeh mih·sah/sloo·zhbah* |

## ESSENTIAL

| | |
|---|---|
| Where is the market/ | **Gdje je tržnica/trgovački centar?** |
| mall [shopping centre]? | gdyeh yeh tr·zhnih·tsah/tr·goh·vah·chkih tsehn·tahr |
| I'm just looking. | **Samo razgledam.** sah·moh rahz·gleh·dahm |
| Can you help me? | **Možete li mi pomoći?** |
| | moh·zheh·teh lih mih poh·moh·chih |
| I'm being helped. | **Već sam uslužen m/uslužena f.** |
| | vehch sahm oo·sloo·zhehn/oo·sloo·zheh·nah |
| How much? | **Koliko?** koh·lih·koh |
| That one, please. | **To, molim Vas.** toh moh·lihm vahs |
| That's all. | **To je sve.** toh yeh sveh |
| Where can I pay? | **Gdje mogu platiti?** gdyeh moh·goo plah·tih·tih |
| I'll pay in cash/ | **Plaćam gotovinom/kraditnom karticom.** |
| by credit card. | plah·chahm goh·toh·vih·nohm/kreh·diht·nohm |
| | kahr·tih·tsohm |
| A receipt, please. | **Račun, molim Vas.** rah·choon moh·lihm vahs |

## At the Shops

| | |
|---|---|
| Where's…? | **Gdje je…?** gdyeh yeh… |
| the antiques store | **antikvarijat** ahn·tih·kvah·rih·yaht |
| the bakery | **pekarnica** peh·kahr·nih·tsah |
| the bank | **banka** bahn·kah |
| the bookstore | **knjižara** knyih·zhah·rah |
| the clothing store | **prodavaonica odjeće** |
| | proh·dah·vah·oh·nih·tsah oh·dyeh·cheh |
| the delicatessen | **delikatesna radnja** deh·lih·kah·teh·snah rah·dnyah |

| | |
|---|---|
| the department store | **robna kuća** *roh·bnah koo·chah* |
| the electronics store | **trgovina elektroničkom robom** *trgoh·vih·nah ehleh·ktroh·nich·kohm roh·bohm* |
| the gift shop | **darovni dućan** *dah·roh·vni doo·chahn* |
| the health food store | **prodavaonica zdrave hrane** *proh·dah·vah·oh·nih·tsah zdrah·veh hrah·neh* |
| the jeweler | **zlatarnica** *zlah·tahr·nih·tsah* |
| the liquor store [off-licence] | **prodavaonica pića** *proh·dah·vah·oh·nih·tsah pih·chah* |
| the market | **tržnica** *tr·zhnih·tsah* |
| the music store | **glazbena prodavaonica** *glah·zbeh·nah proh·dah·vah·oh·nih·tsah* |
| the pastry shop | **slastičarnica** *slah·stih·chahr·nih·tsah* |
| the pharmacy [chemist] | **ljekarna** *lyeh·kahr·nah* |
| the produce [grocery] store | **trgovina mješovite robe** *tr·goh·vih·nah myeh·shoh·vih·teh roh·beh* |
| the shoe store | **prodavaonica obuće** *proh·dah·vah·oh·nih·tsah oh·boo·cheh* |
| the shopping mall | **trgovački centar** *tr·goh·vah·chkih tsehn·tahr* |

| the souvenir store | **suvenirnica** *soo·veh·nihr·nih·tsah* |
| the supermarket | **supermarket** *soo·pehr·mahr·keht* |
| the tobacconist | **trafika** *trah·fih·kah* |
| the toy store | **prodavaonica igračaka** *proh·dah·vah·oh·nih·tsah ih·grah·chah·kah* |

## Ask an Assistant

| When do you open/close? | **Kada otvarate/zatvarate?** *kah·dah oh·tvah·rah·teh/zah·tvah·rah·teh* |
| Where's…? | **Gdje je…?** *gdyeh yeh…* |
| the cashier | **kasa** *kah·sah* |
| the escalator | **pokretne stepenice** *poh·kreh·tneh steh·peh·nih·tseh* |
| the elevator [lift] | **lift** *lihft* |
| the fitting room | **kabina za presvlačenje** *kah·bih·nah zah preh·svlah·cheh·nyeh* |
| the store directory | **uprava trgovine** *oo·prah·vah tr·goh·vih·neh* |
| Can you help me? | **Možete li mi pomoći?** *moh·zheh·teh lih mih poh·moh·chih* |
| I'm just looking. | **Samo razgledavam.** *sah·moh rahz·gleh·dahm* |
| I'm being helped. | **Već sam uslužen** *m*/**uslužena** *f.* *vehch sahm oo·sloo·zhehn/oo·sloo·zheh·nah* |
| Do you have…? | **Imate li…?** *ih·mah·teh lih…* |
| Can you show me…? | **Možete li mi pokazati…?** *moh·zheh·teh lih mih poh·kah·zah·tih…* |
| Can you ship/wrap it? | **Možete li ubaciti/umotati to?** *moh·zheh·teh lih oo·bah·cih·tih/oo·moh·tah·tih toh* |
| How much? | **Koliko?** *koh·lih·koh* |
| That's all. | **To je sve.** *toh yeh sveh* |

For Souvenirs, see page 128.

## YOU MAY HEAR...

**Mogu li Vam pomoći?**      Can I help you?
*moh·goo lih vahm poh·moh·chih*

**Samo trenutak.** *sah·moh treh·noo·tahk*    One moment.

**Što želite?** *shtoh zheh·lih·teh*     What would you like?

**Još nešto?** *yohsh neh·shtoh*     Anything else?

## YOU MAY SEE...

| | |
|---|---|
| OTVORENO/ZATVORENO | open/closed |
| KABINA ZA PRESVLAČENJE | fitting room |
| KASA | cashier |
| SAMO GOTOVINSKO PLAĆANJE | cash only |
| PRIMAMO KREDITNE KARTICE | credit cards accepted |
| UZLAZ/IZLAZ | entrance/exit |
| PAUZA ZA RUČAK | closed for lunch |
| RADNO VRIJEME | opening hours |

### Personal Preferences

| | | |
|---|---|---|
| ThI'd like something... | **Htio *m*/Htjela *f* bih nešto...** | |
| | *htih·oh/htyeh·lah bih neh·shtoh...* | |
| cheap/expensive | **jeftino/skupo** *yeh·ftih·noh/skoo·poh* | |
| larger/smaller | **veće/manje** *veh·cheh/mah·nyeh* | |
| nicer | **ljepše** *lyeh·psheh* | |
| from this region | **s ovog područja** *soh·vohg poh·droo·chyah* | |
| Around...kuna. | **Oko...kuna.** *oh·koh...koo·nah* | |
| Is it real? | **Je li to original?** *yeh lih toh ohr·gih·nah* | |

| Can you show me this/that? | **Možete li mi pokazati ovo/to?** *moh·zheh·teh lih mih poh·kah·zah·tih oh·voh/toh* |
|---|---|
| That's not quite what I want. | **To nije baš ono što želim.** *toh nih·yeh bahsh oh·noh shtoh zheh·lihm* |
| No, I don't like it. | **Ne, to mi se ne sviđa.** *neh, toh mih seh neh svih·jah* |
| I have to think about it. | **Moram razmisliti.** *moh·rahm rah·zmih·slih·tih* |
| I'll take it. | **Kupit ću.** *koo·piht choo* |

## Paying & Bargaining

| That's too much. | **To je previše.** *toh yeh preh·vih·sheh* |
|---|---|
| I'll give you… | **Dat ću Vam…** *daht choo vahm…* |
| I have only…kuna. | **Imam samo…kuna.** *ih·mahm sah·moh…koo·nah* |
| Is that your best price? | **Je li to najniža cijena?** *yeh lih toh nahy·nih·zhah tsih·yeh·nah* |
| Can you give me a discount? | **Možete li mi dati popust?** *moh·zheh·teh lih mih dah·tih poh·poost* |
| How much? | **Koliko?** *koh·lih·koh* |
| I'll pay… | **Platit ću…** *plah·tiht choo…* |
| in cash | **gotovinom** *goh·toh·vih·nohm* |
| by credit card | **kreditnom karticom** *kreh·dih·tnohm kahr·tih·tsohm* |
| by travelers check [cheque] | **putničkim čekovima** *poot·nih·chkihm cheh·koh·vih·mah* |

Can I use this…card? **Mogu li platiti…karticom?**
*moh·goo lih plah·tih·tih…kahr·tih·tsohm*

| | | |
|---|---|---|
| ATM | **bankomat** | *bahn·koh·maht* |
| credit | **kreditnom** | *kreh·dih·tnohm* |
| debit | **debitnom** | *deh·bih·tnohm* |
| gift | **poklon** | *poh·klohn* |

A receipt, please. **Račun, molim Vas.** *rah·choon moh·lihm vahs*

For Numbers, see page 169.

Most major credit cards are accepted in hotels, restaurants and shops. Travelers checks are not accepted everywhere. Personal checks are not accepted. Cash is the preferred method of payment.

### YOU MAY HEAR…

**Čime plaćate?** *chih·meh plah·chah·teh*  How are you paying?

**Ne primamo kreditne kartice.**  We don't accept
*neh prih·mah·moh kreh·dih·tneh kahr·tih·tseh*  credit cards.

**Samo gotovinsko plaćanje, molim Vas.**  Cash only, please.
*sah·moh goh·toh·vihn·skoh*
*plah·chah·nyeh moh·lihm vahs*

## Making a Complaint

| | | |
|---|---|---|
| I'd like… | **Htio** *m*/**Htjela** *f* **bih…** | *htih·oh/htyeh·lah bih…* |
| to exchange this | **zamijeniti to** | *zah·mih·yeh·nih·tih toh* |
| a refund | **povrat novca** | *poh·vraht nohv·tsah* |
| to see the manager | **razgovarati s poslovođom** | |
| | *rah·zgoh·vah·rah·tih s poh·sloh·voh·johm* | |

## Services

| | |
|---|---|
| Can you recommend…? | **Možete li mi preporučiti…?** *moh·zheh·teh lih mih preh·poh·roo·chih·tih…* |
| a barber | **brijačnicu** *brih·yah·chnih·tsoo* |
| a dry cleaner | **kemijsku čistionicu** *keh·mihy·skoo chih·stih·oh·nih·tsoo* |
| a hairstylist | **frizera** *frih·zeh·rah* |
| a laundromat [launderette] | **praonicu** *prah·oh·nih·tsoo* |
| a nail salon | **kozmetički salon** *koh·zmeh·tih·chkih sah·lohn* |
| a spa | **spa** *spah* |
| a travel agency | **putničku agenciju** *poot·nih·chkoo ah·gehn·tsih·yoo* |
| Can you…this? | **Možete li…to?** *moh·zheh·teh lih…toh* |
| alter | **promijeniti** *proh·mih·yeh·nih·tih* |
| clean | **očistiti** *oh·chih·stih·tih* |
| fix [mend] | **popraviti** *poh·prah·vih·tih* |
| press | **izglačati** *ihz·glah·chah·tih* |
| When will it be ready? | **Kada će biti gotovo?** *kah·dah cheh bih·tih goh·toh·voh* |

## Hair & Beauty

| | | |
|---|---|---|
| I'd like… | **Htio** *m*/**Htjela** *f* **bih…** | *htih·oh/htyeh·lah bih…* |
| an appointment for | **se naručiti za danas/sutra seh** | |
| today/tomorrow | | *nah·roo·chih·tih zah dah·nahs/soo·trah* |
| an eyebrow wax | **čupkanje obrva** | *choo·pkah·nyeh oh·br·vah* |
| a bikini wax | **depiliranje prepona voskom** | |
| | | *deh·pih·lih·rah·nyeh preh·poh·nah voh·skohm* |
| a facial | **njegu lica** | *nyeh·goo lih·tsah* |
| a manicure/ | **manikuru/pedikuru** | |
| a pedicure | | *mah·nih·koo·roo/peh·dih·koo·roo* |
| a (sports) massage | **(sportsku) masažu** | *(spohrt·skoo) mah·sah·zhoo* |
| some color/ | **farbanje/pramenove** | |
| highlights | | *fahr·bah·nyeh/prah·meh·noh·veh* |
| my hair styled/ | **friziranje/feniranje** | |
| blow-dried | | *frih·zih·rah·nyeh/feh·nih·rah·nyeh* |
| a haircut | **šišanje** | *shih·shah·nyeh* |
| a trim | **skraćivanje** | *skrah·chih·vah·nyeh* |
| Not too short. | **Ne prekratko.** | *ne preh·krah·tkoh* |
| Shorter here. | **Ovjde kraće.** | *ohv·dyeh krah·cheh* |
| Do you offer…? | **Radite li…?** | *rah·dih·teh lih…* |
| acupuncture | **akupunkturu** | *ah·koo·poon·ktoo·roo* |
| aromatherapy | **aroma-terapiju** | *ah·roh·mah teh·rah·pih·yoo* |
| oxygen treatment | **kisik-terapiju** | *kih·sihk teh·rah·pih·yoo* |
| Do you have a sauna? | **Imate saunu?** | *ih·mah·teh sah·oo·noo* |

## Antiques

| | | |
|---|---|---|
| How old is this? | **Koliko je staro?** | *koh·lih·koh yeh stah·roh* |
| Do you have anything | **Imate li nešto iz…razdoblja?** | |
| from the…period? | | *ih·mah·teh lih neh·shtoh ihz…rahz·doh·blyah* |
| Do I have to fill out | **Moram li popuniti neke obrazce?** | |
| any forms? | | *moh·rahm lih poh·poo·nih·tih neh·keh ohb·rahz·tseh* |

122

| | |
|---|---|
| Is there a certificate of authenticity? | **Imate li uvjerenje o autentičnosti?** *ih·mah lih oo·vyeh·reh·nyeh oah·oo·tehn·tih·chnoh·stih* |
| Can you ship/wrap it? | **Možete li ubaciti/umotati to?** *moh·zheh·teh lih oo·bah·cih·tih/oo·moh·tah·tih toh* |

## Clothing

| | |
|---|---|
| I'd like… | **Htio *m*/Htjela *f* bih…** *htih·oh/htyeh·lah bih…* |
| Can I try this on? | **Mogu li to oprobati?** *moh·goo lih toh oh·proh·bah·tih* |
| It doesn't fit. | **Ne odgovara mi.** *neh ohd·goh·vah·rah mih* |
| It's too… | **To je…** *toh yeh…* |
| big/small | **preveliko/premalo** *preh·veh·lih·koh/preh·mah·loh* |
| short/long | **prekratko/predugo** *preh·krah·tkoh/preh·doo·goh* |
| tight/loose | **preusko/preširoko** *preh·oo·skoh/preh·shih·roh·koh* |
| Do you have this in size…? | **Imate li to veličine…?** *ih·mah·teh lih toh veh·lih·chih·neh…* |
| Do you have this in a bigger/smaller size? | **Imate li to većeg/manjeg broja?** *ih·mah·teh lih toh veh·chehg/mah·nyehg broh·yah* |

For Numbers, see page 169.

**YOU MAY HEAR...**

| | |
|---|---|
| **Dobro Vam pristaje.** | That looks great on you. |
| *doh·broh vahm prih·stah·yeh* | |
| **Kako Vam odgovara?** | How does it fit? |
| *kah·koh vahm ohd·goh·vah·rah* | |
| **Nemamo Vaš broj.** *neh·mah·moh vahsh brohy* | We don't have your size. |

**YOU MAY SEE...**

| | |
|---|---|
| **ODJEL ZA MUŠKARCE** | men's clothing |
| **ODJEL ZA ŽENE** | women's clothing |
| **ODJEL ZA DJECU** | children's clothing |

## Colors

| I'd like something... | **Htio *m*/Htjela *f* bih nešto...** |
|---|---|
| | *htih·oh/htyeh·lah bih neh·shtoh...* |
| beige | **bež** *behzh* |
| black | **crno** *tsr·noh* |
| blue | **plavo** *plah·voh* |
| brown | **smeđe** *smeh·jeh* |
| green | **zeleno** *zeh·leh·noh* |
| gray | **sivo** *sih·voh* |
| orange | **narančasto** *nah·rahn·chah·stoh* |
| pink | **ružičasto** *roo·zhih·chah·stoh* |
| purple | **ljubičasto** *lyoo·bih·chah·stoh* |
| red | **crveno** *tsr·veh·noh* |
| white | **bijelo** *bih·yeh·loh* |
| yellow | **žuto** *zhoo·toh* |

## Clothes & Accessories

| | |
|---|---|
| backpack | **ruksak** *rook·sahk* |
| belt | **remen** *reh·mehn* |
| bikini | **bikini** *bih·kih·nih* |
| blouse | **bluza** *bloo·zah* |
| bra | **grudnjak** *grood·nyahk* |
| briefs [underpants] | **gaćice** *gah·chih·tseh* |
| coat | **kaput** *kah·poot* |
| dress | **haljina** *hah·lyih·nah* |
| hat | **šešir** *sheh·shihr* |
| jacket | **jakna** *yah·knah* |
| jeans | **traperice** *trah·peh·rih·tseh* |
| pajamas [pyjamas] | **pidžama** *pih·jah·mah* |
| pants [trousers] | **hlače** *hlah·cheh* |
| panties [womens] | **gaćice** *gah·chih·tseh* |
| pantyhose [tights] | **hulahopke** *hoo·lah·hohp·keh* |
| purse [handbag] | **torbica** *tohr·bih·tsah* |
| raincoat | **vjetrovka** *vyeh·trohv·kah* |
| scarf | **šal** *shahl* |
| shirt | **košulja** *koh·shoo·lyah* |
| shorts | **kratke hlače** *krah·tkeh hlah·cheh* |

| skirt | **suknja** *sook·nyah* |
| socks | **čarape** *chah·rah·peh* |
| suit | **odijelo** *oh·dih·yeh·loh* |
| sunglasses | **sunčane naočale** *soon·chah·neh nah·oh·chah·leh* |
| sweater | **džemper** *jehm·peh* |
| swimsuit | **kupaći kostim** *koo·pah·chih koh·stihm* |
| T-shirt | **majica** *mah·yih·tsah* |
| tie | **kravata** *krah·vah·tah* |
| underwear | **donje rublje** *doh·nyeh roob·lyeh* |
| womens underwear | **žensko rublje** *zhen·skoh roob·lyeh* |

## Fabric

| I'd like… | **Htio** *m*/**Htjela** *f* **bih nešto…** *htih·oh/htyeh·lah bih neh·shtoh…* |
| cotton | **pamučno** *pah·moo·chnoh* |
| denim | **od trapera** *ohd trah·peh·rah* |
| lace | **čipkasto** *chihp·kah·stoh* |
| leather | **kožno** *koh·zhnoh* |
| linen | **laneno** *lah·neh·noh* |
| silk | **svileno** *svih·leh·noh* |
| wool | **vuneno** *voo·neh·noh* |
| Is it machine washable? | **Pere li se u perilici?** *peh·reh lih seh oo peh·rih·lih·tsih* |

## Shoes

| I'd like… | **Htio** *m*/**Htjela** *f* **bih…** *htih·oh/htyeh·lah bih…* |
| high-heels/flats | **visoke potpetice/ravne cipele** *vih·soh·keh poht·peh·tih·tseh/rahv·neh tsih·peh·leh* |
| boots | **čizme** *chih·zmeh* |
| flip-flops | **japanke** *yah·pahn·keh* |
| hiking boots | **gojzerice** *gohy·zeh·rih·tseh* |
| loafers | **mokasinke** *moh·kah·sihn·keh* |

| | | |
|---|---|---|
| sandals | **sandale** | sahn·dah·leh |
| shoes | **cipele** | tsih·peh·leh |
| slippers | **papuče** | pah·poo·cheh |
| sneakers | **tenisice** | teh·nih·sih·tseh |
| Size… | **Broj…** | brohy… |

For Numbers, see page 169.

## Sizes

| | | |
|---|---|---|
| small (S) | **S** | ehs |
| medium (M) | **M** | ehm |
| large (L) | **L** | ehl |
| extra large (XL) | **XL** | ihks·ehl |
| petite (clothes size) | **male veličine (veličina odjeće)** | mah·leh veh·lih·chih·neh (veh·lih·chih·nah oh·dyeh·cheh) |
| plus size | **veće veličine** | veh·cheh veh·lih·chih·neh |

## Newsagent & Tobacconist

| | | |
|---|---|---|
| Do you sell English language newspapers? | **Imate li novine na engleskom jeziku?** | ih·mah·teh lih noh·vih·neh nah ehn·gleh·skohm yeh·zih·koo |
| I'd like… | **Htio m/Htjela f bih…** | htih·oh/htyeh·lah bih… |
| candy [sweets] | **bombon** | bombon |
| chewing gum | **žvakaća** | guma |

| a cigar | **cigaru** *tsih·gah·roo* |
| a pack/carton of cigarettes | **kutiju/šteku cigareta** *koo·tih·yoo/shteh·koo tsih·gah·reh·tah* |
| a lighter | **upaljač** *oo·pah·lyahch* |
| a magazine | **časopis** *chah·soh·pihs* |
| matches | **šibice** *shih·bih·tseh* |
| a newspaper | **novine** *noh·vih·neh* |
| a pen | **olovka** *olovkah* |
| a postcard | **razglednicu** *rahz·gleh·dnih·tsoo* |
| a road/town map of... | **autokartu/kartu grada...** *ah·oo·toh·kahr·too/kahr·too grah·dah...* |
| stamps | **poštanske markice** *poh·shtahn·skeh mahr·kih·tseh* |

## Photography

| I'd like...camera. | **Htio** *m*/**Htjela** *f* **bih...fotoaparat.** *htih·oh/htyeh·lah bih...foh·toh·ah·pah·raht* |
| an automatic | **automatski** *ah·oo·toh·maht·skih* |
| a digital | **digitalni** *dih·gih·tahl·nih* |
| a disposable | **za jednokratnu uporabu** *zah yeh·dnoh·krah·tnoo oo·poh·rah·boo* |
| I'd like... | **Htio** *m*/**Htjela** *f* **bih...** *htih·oh/htyeh·lah bih...* |
| a battery | **bateriju** *bah·teh·rih·yoo* |
| digital prints | **digitalnu izradu** *dih·gih·tahl·noo ihz·rah·doo* |
| a memory card | **memorijsku karticu** *meh·moh·rihy·skoo kahr·tih·tsoo* |
| Can I print digital photos here? | **Je li mogu ovdje izraditi digitalne fotografije?** *yeh lih moh·goo ohv·dyeh ihz·rah·dih·tih dih·gih·tahl·neh foh·toh·grah·fih·yeh* |

## Souvenirs

| a bottle of wine | **boca vina** *boh·tsah vih·nah* |
| cheese from the island of Pag | **paški sir** *pah·shkih sihr* |

| coral | **morski koralj** *mohr·skih koh·rahly* |
| dried figs | **sušene smokve** *soo·sheh·neh smoh·kveh* |
| dried lavender | **sušena lavanda** *soo·sheh·nah lah·vahn·dah* |
| essential oils | **eterična ulja** *eh·teh·rih·chnah oo·lyah* |
| key ring | **privjesak za ključeve** *prih·vyeh·sahk zah klyoo·cheh·veh* |
| lace from the island of Pag | **paška čipka** *pah·shkah chih·pkah* |
| maraschino liqueur | **liker Maraskino** *lih·kehr mah·rah·skih·noh* |
| olive oil | **maslinovo ulje** *mah·slih·noh·voh oo·lyeh* |
| postcard | **razglednica** *rah·zgleh·dnih·tsah* |
| pottery | **lončarski predmeti** *lohn·chahr·skih preh·dmeh·tih* |
| silk tie | **kravata** *krah·vah·tah* |
| T-shirt | **majica** *mah·yih·tsah* |
| toy | **igračka** *ih·grah·chkah* |
| Can I see this/that? | **Mogu li pogledati to/ovo?** *moh·goo lih poh·gleh·dah·tih toh/oh·voh* |
| It's in the window/ display case. | **U izlogu/vitrini je.** *oo ihz·loh·goo/vih·trih·nih yeh* |
| I'd like… | **Htio** *m/***Htjela** *f* **bih…** *htih·oh/htyeh·lah bih…* |
| a battery | **bateriju** *bah·teh·rih·yoo* |

| | | |
|---|---|---|
| a bracelet | **narukvicu** | *nah·rook·vih·tsoo* |
| a brooch | **broš** | *brohsh* |
| a clock | **sat** | *saht* |
| earrings | **naušnice** | *nah·oosh·nih·tseh* |
| a necklace | **ogrlicu** | *oh·gr·lih·tsoo* |
| a ring | **prsten** | *pr·stehn* |
| a watch | **ručni sat** | *roo·chnih saht* |
| I'd like it made of… | **Htio m/Htjela f bih od…** | *htih·oh/htyeh·lah bih ohd..* |
| copper | **bakra** | *bah·krah* |
| crystal | **kristala** | *krih·stah·lah* |
| cut glass | **brušenog stakla** | *broo·sheh·nohg stah·klah* |
| diamonds | **dijamanata** | *dih·yah·mah· nah·tah* |
| enamel | **emajla** | *eh·mahy·lah* |
| white/yellow gold | **bijelog/žutog zlata** | *bih·yeh·lohg/zhoo·tohg zlah·tah* |
| pearls | **bisera** | *bih·seh·rah* |
| pewter | **kositra** | *koh·sih·trah* |
| platinum | **platine** | *plah·tih·neh* |
| sterling silver | **srebra** | *sreh·brah* |
| Is this real? | **Je li pravo?** | *yeh lih prah·voh* |
| Is there a certificate for it? | **Imate li potvrdu za to?** *ih·mah·teh lih poh·tvr·doo zah toh* | |
| Can you engrave it? | **Možete li urezati?** *moh·zheh·teh lih oo·reh·zah·tih* | |

130

---

Souvenirs can be purchased in **suvenirnica** (souvenir shops) and from stands in most touristy areas. Handmade silk ties, local wine, brandy or maraschino liqueur, olive oil and **paški sir**, the famous Croatian sheep's cheese, all make wonderful souvenirs, as does **Paška čipka** (authentic lacework from the island of Pag).

## ESSENTIAL

| | | |
|---|---|---|
| When's the game? | **Kada je utakmica?** | *kah·dah yeh oo·tah·kmih·tsah* |
| Where's…? | **Gdje je…?** | *gdyeh yeh…* |
| the beach | **plaža** | *plah·zhah* |
| the park | **park** | *pahrk* |
| the pool | **bazen** | *bah·zehn* |
| Is it safe to swim here? | **Je li sigurno kupati se ovdje?** | |
| | *yeh llih sih·goor·noh koo·pah·tih seh ohv·dyeh* | |
| Can I rent [hire] golf clubs? | **Mogu li iznajmiti palice za golf?** | |
| | *moh·goo lih ihz·nahy·mih·tih pah·lih·tseh zah gohlf* | |
| How much per hour? | **Koliko košta po satu?** | |
| | *koh·lih·koh koh·shtah poh sah·too* | |
| How far is it to…? | **Koliko je daleko od…?** | |
| | *koh·lih·koh yeh dah·leh·koh ohd…* | |
| Show me on the map, please. | **Pokažite mi na karti, molim Vas.** | |
| | *poh·kah·zhih·teh mih nah kahr·tih moh·lihm vahs* | |

## Watching Sport

| | | |
|---|---|---|
| When's…game/ match? | **Kada je…utakmica/meč?** | |
| | *ah·dah yeh…oo·tahk·mih·tsah/mehch* | |
| the basketball | **košarkaška** | *koh·shahr·kah* |
| the boxing | **boks** | *bohks* |
| the golf | **golf** | *gohlf* |
| the soccer [football] | **nogometna** | *noh·goh·meht·nah* |
| the tennis | **tenis** | *teh·nis* |
| Where's the racetrack/ stadium? | **Gdje je hipodrom/stadion?** | |
| | *gdyeh yeh hih·poh·drohm/stah·dih·ohn* | |

Nogomet (soccer) is the most widely enjoyed sport. Other popular sports are handball, basketball, tennis, water polo, rowing and swimming. Gambling and betting are also popular, and there are casinos around the country but the only racetracks are in Zagreb.

| | | |
|---|---|---|
| Where can I place a bet? | **Gdje se mogu kladiti?** | *gdyeh seh moh·goo klah·dih·tih* |

## Playing Sport

| | | |
|---|---|---|
| Where is/are…? | **Gdje je/su…?** | *gdyeh yeh/soo…* |
| the golf course | **golfski teren** | *gohlf·skih teh·rehn* |
| the gym | **teretana** | *teh·reh·tah·nah* |
| the park | **park** | *pahrk* |
| the tennis courts | **teniski tereni** | *teh·nih·skih teh·reh·nih* |
| How much per…? | **Koliko košta po…?** | *koh·lih·koh koh·shtah poh…* |
| day | **danu** | *dah·noo* |
| hour | **satu** | *sah·too* |
| game | **partiji** | *pahr·tih·yih* |
| How much per round? | **Koliko za rundu?** | *koh·lih·koh zah roon·doo* |
| Can I rent [hire]…? | **Mogu li iznajmiti…?** | *moh·goo lih ihz·nahy·mih·tih…* |

| golf clubs | **palice za golf** *pah·lih·tseh zah gohlf* |
| equipment | **opremu** *oh·preh·moo* |
| a racket | **reket** *reh·keht* |

## At the Beach/Pool

| Where's the beach/pool? | **Gdje je plaža/bazen?** *gdyeh yeh plah·zhah/bah·zehn* |
| Is there…? | **Ima li…?** *ih·mah lih…* |
| a kiddie [paddling] pool | **bazen za djecu** *bah·zehn zah dyeh·tsoo* |
| an indoor/pool | **zatvoreni/otvoreni bazen** *zah·tvoh·reh·nih/oh·tvoh·reh·nih bah·zehn* |
| a lifeguard | **spasavalac** *spah·sah·vah·lahts* |
| Is it safe…? | **Je li sigurno…?** *yeh lih sih·goor·noh…* |
| to swim | **plivati** *plih·vah·tih* |
| to dive | **roniti** *roh·nih·tih* |
| for children | **za djecu** *zah dyeh·tsoo* |
| I'd like to rent [hire]… | **Htio *m*/Htjela *f* bih iznajmiti…** *htih·oh/htyeh·lah bih ihz·nahy·mih·tih…* |
| a deck chair | **ležaljku** *leh·zhahly·koo* |
| diving equipment | **ronilačku opremu** *roh·nih·lah·chkoo oh·preh·moo* |
| a jet ski | **jet ski** *jeht skih* |
| a motorboat | **motorni čamac** *moh·tohr·nih chah·mahts* |
| a rowboat | **čamac na vesla** *chah·mahts nah veh·slah* |
| snorkeling equipment | **oprema za plitko ronjenje** *oh·preh·mah zah plih·tkoh roh·nyeh·nyeh* |
| a surfboard | **dasku za surfanje** *dah·skoo zah soor·fah·nyeh* |
| a towel | **ručnik** *roo·chnihk* |
| an umbrella | **suncobran** *soon·coh·brahn* |
| water skis | **skije za vodu** *skih·yeh zah voh·doo* |
| a windsurfer | **jedrenje** *dah·skoo zah yeh·dreh·nyeh* |
| For…hours. | **Za…sata.** *zah…sah·tah* |

Croatia is known for its beautiful beaches. The beaches of
Makarska Riviera are among the most stunning in the Adriatic.
Makarska Riviera is especially suitable for families with children. The
Croatian coastline is also dotted with smaller rocky "beaches" formed
from limestone; these are much less frequented and offer a calm respite.

## Winter Sports

| | |
|---|---|
| A lift pass for a day/ five days, please. | **Ski-pass za jedan dan/pet dana, molim Vas.** *skih·pahs zah yeh·dahn dahn/peht dah·nah moh·lihm vahs* |
| I'd like to rent [hire]... | **Htio** *m*/**Htjela** *f* **bih iznajmiti...** *htih·oh/htyeh·lah bih ihz·nahy·mih·tih* |
| boots | **čizme** *chih·zmeh* |
| a helmet | **kacigu** *kah·tsih·goo* |
| poles | **štapove** *shtah·poh·veh* |
| skis | **skije** *skih·yeh* |
| a snowboard | **snowboard** *snoh·bohrd* |
| These are too big/small. | **Ove su mi prevelike/premale.** *oh·veh soo mih preh·veh·lih·keh/preh·mah·leh* |
| Are there lessons? | **Dajete li poduku?** *dah·yeh·teh lih poh·doo·koo* |
| I'm a beginner. | **Ja sam početnik.** *yah sahm poh·cheh·tnihk* |
| I'm experienced. | **Imam iskustva.** *ih·mahm ihs·koos·tvah* |
| A trail [piste] map, please. | **Kartu s pistama, molim Vas.** *kahr·too s pih·stah·mah moh·lihm vahs* |

Two popular skiing locations are **Bjelolasica**, where the
Croatian Olympic Center is located, and **Sljeme**, north of Zagreb.

## YOU MAY SEE...

| | |
|---|---|
| **VUČNICA** | drag lift |
| **ŽIČARA** | cable car |
| **USPINJAČA** | chair lift |
| **POČETNIK** | novice |
| **SREDNJI STUPANJI** | intermediate |
| **EKSPERT** | expert |
| **PISTA ZATVORENA** | trail [piste] closed |

## Out in the Country

A map of..., please.     **Zemljopisnu kartu..., molim Vas.**
*zeh·mlyoh·pihs·noo kahr·too...moh·lihm vahs*

this region     **regije** *reh·gih·yeh*

the walking routes     **staza za pješake** *stah·zah zah pyeh·shah·keh*

the bike routes     **staza za bicikliste** *stah·zah zah bih·tsih·klih·steh*

the trails     **planinarskih staza** *plah·nih·nahr·skihh stah·zah*

Is it...?     **Je li to...?** *yeh lih toh...*

easy     **lako** *lah·koh*

difficult     **teško** *teh·shkoh*

| far | **daleko** *dah·leh·koh* |
| steep | **strmo** *str·moh* |
| How far is it to…? | **Koliko je daleko do…?** *koh·lih·koh yeh* |
| | *dah·leh·koh doh…* |
| Show me on the | **Pokažite mi na karti, molim Vas.** |
| map, please. | *poh·kah·zhih·teh mih nah kahr·tih moh·lihm vahs* |
| I'm lost. | **Izgubio** *m*/**Izgubila** *f* **sam se.** |
| | *ihz·goo·bih·oh/ihz·goo·bih·lah sahm seh* |
| Where's…? | **Gdje je…?** *gdyeh yeh…* |
| the bridge | **most** *mohst* |
| the cave | **pećina** *peh·chih·nah* |
| the cliff | **litica** *lih·tih·tsah* |
| the forest | **šuma** *shoo·mah* |
| the lake | **jezero** *yeh·zeh·roh* |
| the mountain | **planina** *plah·nih·nah* |
| the nature preserve | **park prirode** *pahrk prih·roh·deh* |
| the overlook [viewpoint] | **vidikovac** *vih·dih·koh·vahts* |
| the park | **park** *pahrk* |
| the path | **put** *poot* |
| the peak | **vrh** *vrh* |
| the picnic area | **piknik-područje** *pihk·nihk poh·droo·chyeh* |
| the pond | **ribnjak** *rihb·nyahk* |
| the river | **rijeka** *rih·yeh·kah* |
| the sea | **more** *moh·reh* |
| the (thermal) spring | **(termalni) izvor** *(tehr·mahl·nih) ihz·vohr* |
| the stream | **potok** *poh·tohk* |
| the valley | **dolina** *doh·lih·nah* |
| the vineyard | **vinograd** *vih·noh·grahd* |
| the waterfall | **vodopad** *voh·doh·pahd* |

## ESSENTIAL

| | |
|---|---|
| What's there to do at night? | **Kakav je noćni život?** _kah·kahv yeh noh·chnih zhih·voht_ |
| Do you have a program of events? | **Imate li program događanja?** _ih·mah·teh lih proh·grahm doh·gah·jah·nyah_ |
| What's playing tonight? | **Tko svira večeras?** _tkoh svih·rah veh·cheh·rahs_ |
| Where's...? | **Gdje je...?** _gdyeh yeh..._ |
| the downtown area | **centar grada** _tsehn·tahr grah·dah_ |
| the bar | **bar** _bahr_ |
| the dance club | **disko klub** _dih·skoh kloob_ |

## Entertainment

| | |
|---|---|
| Can you recommend...? | **Možete li preporučiti...?** _moh·zheh·teh lih preh·poh·roo·chih·tih..._ |
| a ballet | **balet** _bah·leht_ |
| a concert | **koncert** _kohn·tsehrt_ |
| a movie | **film** _fihlm_ |
| an opera | **operu** _oh·peh·roo_ |
| a play | **predstavu** _prehd·stah·voo_ |
| When does it start/end? | **Kada počinje/završava?** _kah·dah poh·chih·nyeh/zah·vr·shah·vah_ |
| Where's...? | **Gdje je...?** _gdyeh yeh..._ |
| the concert hall | **koncertna dvorana** _kohn·tsehr·tnah dvoh·rah·nah_ |
| the opera house | **opera** _oh·peh·rah_ |
| the theater | **kazalište** _kah·zah·lih·shteh_ |
| What's the dress code? | **Kako treba biti obučen?** _kah·koh treh·bah bih·tih oh·boo·chehn_ |

| What's playing tonight? | **ko nastupa večeras?** *tkoh nah·stoo·pah veh·cheh·rahs?* |
| I like... | **Ja volim...** *yah voh·lihm...* |
| classical music | **klasičnu glazbu** *klah·sih·chnoo glahz·boo* |
| folk music | **narodnu glazbu** *nah·roh·dnoo glahz·boo* |
| jazz | **jazz** *jehz* |
| pop music | **pop glazbu** *pohp glahz·boo* |
| rap | **rap** *rehp* |

For Tickets, see page 19.

**Tourist information offices**, travel agencies and local magazines have extensive information regarding events throughout Croatia.

**Dubrovačke ljetne igre** (Dubrovnik Summer Festival), which takes place in July in the old town of Dubrovnik, features an eclectic program of classical music, theater, opera and dance. Palaces, churches and monasteries are some of the locations of the performances.

**International Film Festival Motovun** is held in August in the medieval village of Motovun, located in the center of the Istrian peninsula. **Sinjska alka** is an equestrian medieval game held every August in the town of Sinj and attracts thousands.

## Nightlife

| What's there to do at night? | **Kakav je ovdje noćni život?** *kah·kahv yeh ohv·dyeh noh·chnih zhih·voht* |
| Can you recommend...? | **Možete li preporučiti...?** *moh·zheh·teh lih preh·poh·roo·chih·tih...* |
| a bar | **bar** *bahr* |
| a casino | **kasino** *kah·sih·noh* |

## YOU MAY HEAR...

**Rasprodano je.** *rah·sproh·dah·noh yeh*  We're sold out.

**Gotovinom ili karticom?** *goh·toh·vih·nohm*  Cash or credit?
*ih·lih kahr·tih·tsohm*

**Isključite mobilne telefone, molim Vas.**  Turn off your mobile
*ihs·klyoo·chih·teh moh·bihl·neh*  phones, please.
*teh·leh·foh·neh moh·lihm vahs*

| | |
|---|---|
| a dance club | **disko klub** *dih·skoh kloob* |
| a jazz club | **jazz klub** *jehz kloob* |
| a club with | **klub s hrvatskom glazbom kloob** |
| | *s hr·vaht·skohm glahz·bohm* |
| Is there live music? | **Ima li glazba u živo?** |
| | *ih·mah lih glahz·bah oo zhih·voh* |
| How do I get there? | **Kako mogu doći do tamo?** |
| | *kah·koh moh·goo doh·chih doh tah·moh* |
| Let's go dancing. | **Idemo plesati.** *ih·deh·moh pleh·sah·tih* |
| Is this area safe | **Je li ovaj dio noću siguran?** |
| at night? | *yeh lih oh·vahy dihoh noh·choo sih·goo·rahn* |

# Special Requirements

# Business Travel

## ESSENTIAL

| | |
|---|---|
| I'm here on business. | **Ovdje sam poslovno.** *ohv·dyeh sahm poh·sloh·vnoh* |
| Here's my business card. | **Izvolite moju vizit karticu.** *ihz·voh·lih·teh moh·yoo vih·ziht kahr·tih·tsoo* |
| Can I have your card? | **Mogu li ja dobiti Vašu karticu?** *moh·goo lih ja doh·bih·tih vah·shoo kahr·tih·tsoo* |
| I have a meeting with… | **Imam sastanak sa…** *ih·mahm sah·stah·nahk sah…* |
| Where's the…? | **Gdje je…?** *gdyeh yeh…* |
| business center | **poslovni centar** *poh·sloh·vnih tsehn·tahr* |
| convention hall | **kongresna sala** *kohn·greh·snha sah·lah* |
| meeting room | **prostorija za sastanke** *proh·stoh·rih·yah zah sahs·tahn·keh* |

It is common to greet colleagues with **dobar dan** (good day). Shake hands if it is the first time you are meeting someone in a professional setting, or if it is someone you haven't seen in a while. When leaving, simply say **doviđenja** (goodbye).

## On Business

| | |
|---|---|
| I'm here… | **Ovdje sam…** *ohv·dyeh sahm…* |
| on business | **poslovno** *poh·slohv·noh* |
| for a seminar | **na seminaru** *nah seh·mih·nah·roo* |
| for a conference | **na konferenciji** *nah kohn·feh·rehn·tsih·yih* |
| for a meeting | **na sastanku** *nah sahs·tahn·koo* |

## YOU MAY HEAR...

**Imate li zakazan sastanak?**
*ih·mah·teh lih zah·kah·zahn sah·stah·nahk*
Do you have an appointment?

**S kim?** *skeem*
With whom?

**On/Ona je na sastanku.**
*ohn/oh·nah yeh nah sahs·tahn·koo*
He/She is in a meeting.

**Samo trenutak, molim Vas.**
*sah·moh treh·noo·tahk moh·lihm vahs*
One moment, please.

**Izvolite sjesti.** *ihz·voh·lih·teh syeh·stih*
Have a seat.

**Želite li nešto popiti?**
*zheh·lih·teh lih neh·shtoh poh·pih·tih*
Would you like something to drink?

**Hvala na posjeti.** *hvah·lah nah poh·syeh·tih*
Thank you for coming.

| | |
|---|---|
| My name is... | **Moje ime je...** *moh·yeh ih·meh yeh...* |
| May I introduce my colleague... | **Dopustite da Vam predstavim svoje kolege...** *doh·poo·sti·teh dah vahm prehd·stah·vihm svoh·yeh koh·leh·geh...* |
| I have a meeting/an appointment with... | **Imam zasjedanje/sastanak sa...** *ih·mahm zah·syeh·dah·nyeh/sah·stah·nahk sah...* |
| I'm sorry I'm late. | **Ispričavam se što kasnim.** *ihs·prih·chah·vahm seh shtoh kah·snihm* |
| I need an interpreter. | **Trebam prevoditelja.** *treh·bahm preh·voh·dih·teh·lyah* |
| You can reach me at the...Hotel. | **Možete me naći u hotelu...** *moh·zheh·teh meh nah·chih oo hoh·teh·loo...* |
| I'm here until... | **Tu sam do...** *too sahm doh...* |
| I need to... | **Trebam...** *treh·bahm...* |
| make a call | **telefonirati** *teh·leh·foh·nih·rah·tih* |
| make a photocopy | **nešto fotokopirati** *neh·shtoh foh·toh·koh·pih·rah·tih* |

| send an email | **poslati e-mail** *poh·slah·tih ee·mehyl* |
| scan something | **skenirati nešto** *skeh·nee·rah·tee neh·shtoh* |
| send a package | **poslati paket** *poh·slah·tih pah·keht* |
| It was a pleasure to meet you. | **Bilo mi je zadovoljstvo upoznati Vas.** *bih·loh mih yeh zah·doh·vohly·stvoh oo·poh·znah·tih vahs* |

For Communications, see page 49.

## Traveling with Children

### ESSENTIAL

| Is there a discount for children? | **Ima li popust za djecu?** *ih·mah lih poh·poost zah dyeh·tsoo* |
| Can you recommend a babysitter? | **Možete li mi preporučiti dadilju?** *moh·zheh·teh lih mih preh·poh·roo·chih·tih dah·dih·lyoo* |
| Do you have a child's seat/highchair? | **Imate li sjedalo za djete/stolicu za hranjenje djece?** *ih·mah·teh lih syeh·dah·loh zah dyeh·teh/ stoh·lih·tsoo zah hrah·nyeh·nyeh dyeh·tseh* |
| Where can I change the baby? | **Gdje mogu presvući djete?** *gdyeh moh·goo preh·svoo·chih dyeh·teh* |

### Out & About

| Can you recommend something for kids? | **Možete li preporučiti nešto za djecu?** *moh·zheh·teh lih preh·poh·roo·chih·tih neh·shtoh zah dyeh·tsoo* |
| Where's...? | **Gdje je...?** *gdyeh yeh...* |
| the amusement park | **zabavni park** *zah·bahv·nih pahrk* |
| the arcade | **igraonica** *ih·grah·oh·nih·tsah* |
| the kiddie [paddling] pool | **dječiji bazen** *dyeh·chih·yih bah·zehn* |
| the park | **park** *pahrk* |

**YOU MAY HEAR...**

| | |
|---|---|
| **Baš slatko!** *bash slah·tkoh* | How cute! |
| **Kako se zove?** *kah·koh seh zoh·veh* | What's his/her name? |
| **Koliko mu *m*/joj *f* je godina?** | How old is he/she? |
| *koh·lih·koh moo/yohy yeh goh·dih·nah* | |

| | | |
|---|---|---|
| the playground | **igralište** *ih·grah·lih·shteh* | |
| the zoo | **zoološki vrt** *zoh·oh·loh·shkih vrt* | |
| Are kids allowed? | **Je li dozvoljeno djeci?** | |
| | *yeh lih doh·zvoh·lyeh·noh dyeh·tsih* | |
| Is it safe for kids? | **Je li sigurno za djecu?** *yeh lih sih·goor·noh zah dyeh·tsoo* | |
| Is it suitable for... | **Je li prikladno za...ogodišnjake?** | |
| year olds? | *yeh lih prih·klah·dnoh zah...oh·goh·dih·shnyah·keh* | |

For Numbers, see page 169.

## Baby Essentials

| | | |
|---|---|---|
| Do you have...? | **Imate li...?** *ih·mah·teh lih...* | |
| a baby bottle | **bočicu za bebe** *boh·chih·tsoo zah beh·beh* | |
| baby food | **dječiju hranu** *dyeh·chih·yoo hrah·noo* | |
| baby wipes | **vlažne maramice** *vlah·zhneh mah·rah·mih·tseh* | |
| a car seat | **dječije sjedalo za auto** | |
| | *dyeh·chih·yeh syeh·dah·loh zah ah·oo·toh* | |
| a children's menu/ | **dječiji meni/dječiju porciju** *dyeh·chih·yih meh·nih/* | |
| portion | *dyeh·chih·yoo pohr·tsih·yoo* | |
| a child's seat/ | **sjedalo za djete/stolicu za hranjenje djece** | |
| a highchair | *syeh·dah·loh zah dyeh·teh/stoh·lih·tsoo zah* | |
| | *hrah·nyeh·nyeh dyeh·tseh* | |
| a crib/a cot | **dječiji krevetić/kolijevka** | |
| | *dyeh·chih·yih kreh·veh·tihch/koh·lih·yehv·kah* | |
| diapers [nappies] | **pelene** *peh·leh·neh* | |

| | | |
|---|---|---|
| formula [baby food] | **dječiju hranu** | *dyeh·chih·yoo hrah·noo* |
| a pacifier [soother] | **dudu** | *doo·doo* |
| a playpen | **hodalicu** | *hoh·dah·lih·tsoo* |
| a stroller [pushchair] | **dječija kolica** | *dyeh·chih·yah koh·lih·tsah* |

| | |
|---|---|
| Can I breastfeed the baby here? | **Mogu li dojiti dijete ovdje?** *moh·goo lih doh·yih·tih dih·yeh·teh ohv·dyeh* |
| Where can I breastfeed/change the baby? | **Gdje mogu dojiti/presvući dijete?** *gdyeh moh·goo doh·yih·tih/preh·svoo·chih dih·yeh·teh* |

For Dining with Children, see page 63.

## Babysitting

| | |
|---|---|
| Can you recommend a babysitter? | **Možete li preporučiti dadilju?** *moh·zheh·teh lih preh·poh·roo·chih·tih dah·dih·lyoo* |
| How much do you/they charge? | **Koliko košta?** *koh·lih·koh koh·shtah* |
| Is there constant supervision? | **Je li neprekidan nadzor?** *yeh lih neh·preh·kih·dahn nahd·zohr* |
| I'll be back by... | **Vratit ću se do...** *vrah·tiht choo seh doh...* |
| I can be reached at... | **Možete me dobiti na...** *moh·zheh·teh meh doh·bih·tih nah...* |

For Time, see page 170.

## Health & Emergency

| | |
|---|---|
| Can you recommend a pediatrician? | **Možete li preporučiti pedijatra?** *moh·zheh·teh lih preh·poh·roo·chih·tih peh·dih·yah·trah* |
| My child is allergic to... | **Moje dijete je alergično na...** *moh·yeh dih·yeh·teh yeh ah·lehr·gih·chnoh nah...* |
| My child is missing. | **Moje dijete je nestalo.** *moh·yeh dih·yeh·teh yeh neh·stah·loh* |
| Have you seen a boy/girl? | **Jeste li vidjeli jednog dječaka/jednudjevojčicu?** *yeh·steh lih vih·dyeh·lih yeh·dnohg dyeh·chah·kah/ yeh·dnoo dyeh·vohy·chih·tsoo* |

For Police, see page 150

# Disabled Travelers

## ESSENTIAL

| | |
|---|---|
| Is there...? | **Ima li...?** *ih·mah lih...* |
|   access for the disabled | **prilaz za hendikepirane** *prih·lahz zah hehn·dih·keh·pih·rah·neh* |
|   a wheelchair ramp | **ulaz za invalidska kolica** *oo·lahz zah ihn·vah·lihd·skah koh·lih·tsah* |
|   a disabled-accessible toilet | **zahod za hendikepirane** *zah·hohd zah hehn·dih·keh·pih·rah·neh* |
| I need... | **Treba mi...** *treh·bah mih...* |
|   assistance | **pomoć** *poh·mohch* |
|   an elevator [a lift] | **lift** *lihft* |
|   a ground-floor room | **soba na prizemlju** *soh·bah nah prih·zehm·lyoo* |

## Asking for Assistance

| | |
|---|---|
| I'm... | **Ja sam...** *yah sahm...* |
| disabled | **nepokretan** *m***/nepokretna** *f* |
| | *neh·poh·kreh·tahn/neh·poh·kreh·tnah* |
| visually impaired | **oštećenog vida** *oh·shteh·cheh·nohg vih·dah* |
| hearing impaired | **oštećenog sluha/gluh** |
| /deaf | *oh·shteh·cheh·nohg sloo·hah/glooh* |
| unable to walk far/ | **nesposoban** *m***/nesposobna** *f* **brzo hodati/** |
| use the stairs | **koristiti stepenice** *neh·spoh·soh·bahn/* |
| | *neh·spoh·sohb·nah br·zoh hoh·dah·tih/koh·rih·stih·tih* |
| | *steh·peh·nih·tseh* |
| Please speak louder. | **Molim Vas govorite glasnije.** |
| | *moh·lihm vahs goh·voh·rih·teh glahs·nih·yeh* |
| Can I bring my | **Mogu li doći s invalidskim kolicima?** *moh·goo lih* |
| wheelchair? | *doh·chih sihn·vah·lihd·skihm koh·lih·tsih·mah* |
| Are guide dogs | **Je li dozvoljeno psima vodičima?** |
| permitted? | *yeh lih doh·zvoh·lyeh·noh psih·mah voh·dih·chih·mah* |
| Can you help me? | **Možete li mi pomoći?** |
| | *moh·zheh·teh lih mih poh·moh·chih* |
| Please open/hold | **Molim Vas otvorite/držite vrata.** |
| the door. | *moh·lihm vahs oh·tvoh·rih·teh/dr·zhih·teh vrah·tah* |

For Emergencies, see page 149

# In an Emergency

## ESSENTIAL

| | | |
|---|---|---|
| Help! | **Upomoć!** | *oo·poh·mohch* |
| Go away! | **Odlazi!** | *oh·dlah·zih* |
| Stop thief! | **Stop, lopov!** | *stohp loh·pohv* |
| Get a doctor! | **Dovedite doktora!** | *doh·veh·dih·teh doh·ktoh·rah* |
| Fire! | **Požar!** | *poh·zhahr* |
| I'm lost. | **Izgubio** *m*/**Izgubila** *f* **sam se.** | |
| | *ihz·goo·bih·oh/ihz·goo·bih·lah sahm seh* | |
| Can you help me? | **Možete li mi pomoći?** | |
| | *moh·zheh·teh lih mih poh·moh·chih* | |

In an emergency, dial: 112
For the telephone directory, dial 988.

## YOU MAY HEAR...

| | |
|---|---|
| **Popunite ovaj obrazac.** *poh·poo·nih·teh oh·vahy oh·brah·zahts* | Fill out this form. |
| **Vašu osobnu ispravu, molim** *Vas. vah·shoo oh·soh·bnoo ihs·prah·voo moh·lihm vahs* | Your ID, please. |
| **Kada/Gdje se to dogodilo?** *kah·dah/gdyeh seh toh doh·goh·dih·loh* | When/Where did it happen? |
| **Kako je izgledao** *m*/**izgledala** *f*? *kah·koh yeh ihz·gleh·dah·oh/ihz·gleh·dah·lah* | What does he/ she look like? |

## ESSENTIAL

| | |
|---|---|
| Call the police! | **Zovite policiju!** |
| | *zoh·vih·teh poh·lih·tsih·yoo* |
| Where's the police station? | **Gdje je policijska postaja?** |
| | *gdyeh yeh poh·lih·tsihy·skah poh·stah·yah* |
| There was an accident. | **Dogodila se nezgoda.** |
| | *doh·goh·dih·lah seh neh·zgoh·dah* |
| There was an attack. | **Dogodio se napad.** |
| | *doh·goh·dih·oh seh nah·pahd* |
| My child is missing. | **Moje dijete je nestalo.** |
| | *moh·yeh dyeh·teh yeh neh·stah·loh* |
| I need... | **Trebam...** *treh·bahm...* |
| an interpreter | **prevoditelja** *preh·voh·dih·teh·lyah* |
| to contact my lawyer | **kontaktirati svog odvjetnika** |
| | *kohn·tah·ktih·rah·tih svohg ohd·vyeh·tnih·kah* |
| to make a phone call | **telefonirati** *teh·leh·foh·nih·rah·tih* |
| to contact my consulate | **kontaktirati svoj konzulat** |
| | *kohn·tah·ktih·rah·tih svohy kohn·zoo·laht* |
| I'm innocent. | **Ja sam nevin** *m*/**nevina** *f*. |
| | *yah sahm neh·vihn/neh·vih·nah* |
| I need a police report. | **Treba mi policijski izvještaj.** |
| | *treh·bah mih poh·lih·tsihy·skih ihz·vyeh·shtahy* |
| Where is the British/ American/Irish embassy? | **Gdje je britansko/američko/irsko veleposlanstvo?** *gdyeh yeh brih·tahn·skoh/ ah·meh·rihch·koh/ihr·skoh veh·leh·pohs·lahn·stvoh* |

# Crime & Lost Property

| | | |
|---|---|---|
| I want to report… | **Htio** *m*/**Htjela** *f* **bih prijaviti…** | |
| | *htih·oh/htyeh·lah bih prih·yah·vih·tih…* | |
| a mugging | **napad** *nah·pahd* | |
| a rape | **silovanje** *sih·loh·vah·nyeh* | |
| a theft | **krađu** *krah·joo* | |
| I was mugged. | **Bio sam napadnut** *m*/**Bila sam napadnuta** *f*. | |
| | *bih·oh nah·pah·dnoot//bih·lah sahm nah·pah·dnoo·tah* | |
| I was robbed. | **Bio sam pokraden** *m*/**Bila sam pokradena** *f*. | |
| | *bih·oh sahm poh·krah·dehn/bih·lah sahm* | |
| | *poh·krah·deh·nah* | |
| I lost my… | **Izgubio** *m*/**Izgubila** *f* **sam…** | |
| | *ihz·goo·bih·oh/ihz·goo·bih·lah sahm…* | |
| My…was stolen. | **Moj…je ukraden.** *mohy…yeh oo·krah·dehn* | |
| backpack | **ruksak** *rook·sahk* | |
| bicycle | **bicikl** *bih·cihkl* | |
| camera | **fotoaparat** *foh·toh·ah·pah·raht* | |
| (rental [hire]) car | **(iznajmljeni) auto** *(ihz·nahy·mlyeh·nih) ah·oo·toh* | |
| computer | **računar** *rah·choo·nahr* | |
| credit card | **kraditna kartica** *kreh·diht·nah kahr·tih·tsah* | |
| iPad | **iPad** *i·pad* | |
| jewelry | **nakit** *nah·kiht* | |
| money | **novac** *noh·vahts* | |
| passport | **putovnica** *poo·tohv·nih·tsah* | |
| purse [handbag] | **torbica** *tohr·bih·tsah* | |
| travelers checks [cheques] | **putnički čekovi** *poot·nih·chkih cheh·koh·vih* | |
| wallet | **novčanik** *nohv·chah·nihk* | |

## Health

### ESSENTIAL

| | |
|---|---|
| I'm sick [ill]. | **Bolestan** *m*/**Bolesna** *f* **sam.** |
| | *boh·leh·stahn/boh·leh·snah sahm* |
| I need an English- | **Treba mi doktor koji govori engleski.** *treh·bah* |
| speaking doctor. | *mih dohk·tohr koh·yih goh·voh·rih ehn·gleh·skih* |
| It hurts here. | **Tu me boli.** *too meh boh·lih* |
| I have a stomachache. | **Boli me stomak.** *boh·lih meh stoh·mahk* |
| I have a stomachache. | **Boli me stomak.** *boh·lih meh stoh·mahk* |

### Finding a Doctor

| | |
|---|---|
| Can you recommend | **Možete li preporučiti doktora/zubara?** |
| a doctor/dentist? | *moh·zheh·teh lih preh·poh·roo·chih·tih dohk·toh·rah/* |
| | *zoo·bah·rah* |
| Can the doctor | **Može li doktor doći ovdje?** |
| come here? | *moh·zheh lih dohk·tohr doh·chih ohv·dyeh* |
| I need an English- | **Treba mi doktor koji govori engleski.** |
| speaking doctor. | *treh·bah mih dohk·tohr koh·yih goh·voh·rih ehn·gleh·skih* |
| What are the | **Koje je radno vrijeme?** |
| office hours? | *koh·yeh yeh rah·dnoh vrih·yeh·meh* |
| I'd like an | **Htio** *m*/**Htjela** *f* **bih se naručiti za…** |
| appointment for… | *htih·oh/htyeh·lah bih seh nah·roo·chih·tih za…* |
| today | **danas** *dah·nahs* |
| tomorrow | **sutra** *soo·trah* |
| as soon as possible | **što je prije moguće** *shtoh yeh prih·yeh moh·goo·cheh* |
| It's urgent. | **Hitno je.** *hih·tnoh yeh* |
| I have an appointment | **Naručen** *m*/**Naručena** *f* **sam kod doktora…** |
| with Doctor… | *nah·roo·chehn/nah·roo·cheh·nah sahm kohd* |
| | *dohk·toh·rah…* |

## Symptoms

| | |
|---|---|
| I'm bleeding. | **Krvarim.** kr·vah·rihm |
| I'm constipated. | **Nemam stolicu.** neh·mahm stoh·lih·tsoo |
| I'm dizzy. | **Imam vrtoglavicu.** ih·mahm vr·toh·glah·vih·tsoo |
| I'm nauseous. | **Muka mi je.** moo·kah mih yeh |
| I'm vomiting. | **Povraćam.** poh·vrah·chahm |
| It hurts here. | **Tu me boli.** too meh boh·lih |
| I have... | **Imam...** ih·mahm... |
| an allergic reaction | **alergijsku reakciju** ah·lehr·gihy·skoo reh·ahk·tsih·yoo |
| chest pain | **bol u prsima** bohl oo pr·sih·mah |
| cramps | **grčeve** gr·cheh·veh |
| diarrhea | **proljev** proh·lyehv |
| an earache | **bol u uhu** bohl oo oo·hoo |
| a fever | **vrućicu** vroo·chih·tsoo |
| a rash | **osip** oh·sihp |
| some swelling | **oticanje** oh·tih·tsah·nyeh |
| a sore throat | **grlobolju** gr·loh·boh·lyoo |
| a stomachache | **bol u stomaku** bohl oo stoh·mah·koo |
| sunstroke | **sunčanicu** soon·chah·nih·tsoo |
| I've been sick [ill for...days. | **Bolestan** m/**Bolesna** f **sam već...dana.** boh·leh·stahn/boh·leh·snah sahm vehch...dah·nah |

## Conditions

| | |
|---|---|
| I'm... | **Ja sam...** *jah sahm...* |
| anemic | **anemičan** *m*/**anemična** *f* |
| | *ah·neh·mih·chahn/ah·neh·mih·chnah* |
| asthmatic | **astmatičar** *ahst·mah·tih chahr* |
| diabetic | **dijabatičar** *dih·yah·beh·tih·chahr* |
| I'm epileptic. | **Imam epilepsiju.** *ih·mahm eh·pih·leh·psih·yoo* |
| I'm allergic to | **Alergičan** *m*/**Alergična** *f* **sam na** |
| | *ah·lehr·gih·chahn/ah·lehr·gih·chnah sahm nah* |
| antibiotics/penicillin. | **antibiotike/penicilin.** *ahn·tih·bih·oh·tih·keh/* |
| | *peh·nih·tsih·lihn* |
| I have... | **Imam...** *ih·mahm...* |
| arthritis | **upalu zglobova** *oo·pah·loo zgloh·boh·vah* |
| a heart condition | **bolesno srce** *boh·leh·snoh sr·tseh* |
| high/low blood | **visok/nizak krvni tlak** *vih·sohk/nih·zahk kr·vnih tlahk* |
| pressure | |
| I'm on medication. | **Uzimam lijekove.** *oo·zih·mahm lih·yeh·koh·veh* |
| I'm on... | **Uzimam...** *oo·zih·mahm...* |

For Dietary Requirements, see page 62.

## YOU MAY HEAR...

**Što nije uredu?** *shtoh nih·yeh oo·reh·doo* — What's wrong?

**Gdje Vas boli?** *gdyeh vahs boh·lih* — Where does it hurt?

**Boli li Vas ovdje?** *boh·lih lih vahs ohv·dyeh* — Does it hurt here?

**Uzimete li lijekove?**
*oo·zih·mah·teh lih lih·yeh·koh·veh* — Are you on medication?

**Jeste li na nešto alergični?**
*yeh·steh lih nah neh·shtoh ah·lehr·gih·chnih* — Are you allergic to anything?

**Otvorite usta.** *oh·tvoh·rih·teh oo·stah* — Open your mouth.

**Duboko dišite.** *doo·boh·koh dih·shih·teh* — Breathe deeply.

**Kašljite molim Vas.**
*kah·shlyih·teh moh·lihm vahs* — Cough please.

**Idite kod specijaliste.**
*ih·dih·teh kohd speh·tsih·yah·lih·steh* — See a specialist.

**Idite u bolnicu.** *ih·dih·teh oo bohl·nih·tsoo* — Go to the hospital.

## Treatment

| | |
|---|---|
| Do I need a prescription/medicine? | **Treba li mi recept/liječenje?** *treh·bah lih mih reh·tsehpt/lih·yeh·cheh·nyeh* |
| Can you prescribe a generic drug [unbranded medication]? | **Možete li mi propisati lijek koji se spravlja?** *moh·zheh·teh lih mih proh·pih·sah·tih lih·yehk koh·yih seh sprahv·lyah* |
| Where can I get it? | **Gdje ga mogu nabaviti?** *gdyeh gah moh·goo nah·bah·vih·tih* |

For What to Take, see page 159.

## Hospital

| | |
|---|---|
| Notify my family, please. | **Obavijestite moju obitelj, molim Vas.** *oh·bah·vyeh·stih·teh moh·yoo oh·bih·tehly moh·lihm vahs* |
| I'm in pain. | **Boli me.** *boh·lih meh* |
| I need a doctor/nurse. | **Trebam doktora/medicinsku sestru.** *treh·bahm dohk·toh·rah/meh·dih·tsihn·skoo seh·stroo* |
| When are visiting hours? | **Kada je posjeta?** *kah·dah yeh poh·syeh·tah* |
| I'm visiting… | **Posjećivam…** *poh·syeh·chih·vahm…* |

## Dentist

| | |
|---|---|
| I have… | **Imam…** *ih·mahm…* |
| a broken tooth | **slomljen zub** *sloh·mlyehn zoob* |
| a lost filling | **plombu koja je ispala** *plohm·boo koh·yah yeh ihs·pah·lah* |
| a toothache | **zubobolju** *zoo·boh·boh·lyoo* |
| Can you fix this denture? | **Možete li popraviti ovu zubnu protezu?** *moh·zheh·teh lih poh·prah·vih·tih oh·voo zoo·bnoo proh·teh·zoo* |

## Gynecologist

| | |
|---|---|
| I have cramps/a vaginal infection. | **Imam grčeve/vaginalnu infekciju.** *ih·mahm gr·cheh·veh/vah·gih·nahl·noo ihn·fehk·tsih·yoo* |
| I missed my period. | **Izostala mi je mjesečnica.** *ih·zoh·stah·lah mih yeh myeh·seh·chnih·tsah* |
| I'm on the Pill. | **Uzimam pilule za kontracepciju.** *oo·zih·mahm pih·loo·leh zah kohn·trah·tsehp·tsih·yoo* |
| I'm (…months) pregnant. | **Trudna sam (…mjeseci).** *troo·dnah sahm (…myeh·seh·tsih)* |
| I'm not pregnant. | **Nisam trudna.** *nih·sahm troo·dnah* |
| My last period was… | **Zadnja mjesečnica je bila…** *zah·dnyah myeh·seh·chnih·tsah yeh bih·lah…* |

## Optician

| | |
|---|---|
| I lost… | **Izgubio** *m***/Izgubila** *f* **sam…** |
| | *ihz·goo·bih·oh/ihz·goo·bih·lah sahm…* |
| a contact lens | **kontaktnu leću** *koh·tahk·tnoo leh·choo* |
| my glasses | **naočale** *nah·oh·chah·leh* |
| a lens | **staklo od naočala** *stah·kloh ohd nah·oh·chah·lah* |

## Payment & Insurance

| | |
|---|---|
| How much? | **Koliko?** *koh·lih·koh* |
| Can I pay by credit card? | **Mogu li platiti kreditnom karticom?** |
| | *moh·goo lih plah·tih·tih kreh·diht·nohm kahr·zih·tsohm* |
| I have insurance. | **Imam osiguranje.** *ih·mahm oh·sih·goo·rah·nyeh* |
| I need a receipt for my insurance. | **Treba mi račun za moje osiguranje.** |
| | *treh·bah mih rah·choon zah moh·yeh oh·sih·goo·rah·nyeh* |

## Pharmacy

### ESSENTIAL

| | |
|---|---|
| Where's the pharmacy [chemist]? | **Gdje je ljekarna?** *gdyeh yeh lyeh·kahr·nah* |
| What time does it open/close? | **Kada se otvara/zatvara?** *kah·dah seh oh·tvah·rah/zah·tvah·rah* |
| What would you recommend for…? | **Što biste preporučili za…?** *shtoh bih·steh preh·poh·roo·chih·lih zah…* |
| How much do I take? | **Koliko uzimam?** *koh·lih·koh oo·zih·mahm* |
| Can you fill [make up] this prescription? | **Možete li mi dati to što je propisano?** *moh·zheh·teh lih mih dah·tih toh shtoh yeh proh·pih·sah·noh* |
| I'm allergic to… | **Alergičan** *m***/Alergična** *f* **sam na…** *ah·lehr·gih·chahn /ah·lehr·gih·chnah sahm nah…* |

Pharmacies are open from 8:00 a.m. to 8:00 p.m. on weekdays, and from 8:00 a.m. to 2:00 p.m. on Saturdays. **Dežurne ljekarne** are pharmacies that are open at night or on Sundays. The list of on-duty pharmacies can be found in the windows of pharmacies and is also published in local newspapers. Pharmacists can give medical advice for minor complaints but, for serious problems, go to a hospital or call an ambulance on 112.

## What to Take

| | | |
|---|---|---|
| How much do I take? | **Koliko uzimam?** | koh·lih·koh oo·zih·mahm |
| How often? | **Koliko često?** | koh·lih·koh cheh·stoh |
| Is it safe for children? | **Smiju li djeca uzimati?** | smih·yoo lih dyeh·tsah oo·zih·mah·tih |
| I'm taking… | **Uzimam…** | oo·zih·mahm… |
| Are there side effects? | **Ima li ikakvih nuspojava?** | |
| | | ih·mah lih ih·kah·kvih noos·poh·yah·vah |
| I need something | **Treba mi nešto protiv…** | |
| for… | | treh·bah mih neh·shtoh proh·tihv… |
| a cold | **hunjavice** | hoo·nyah·vih·tseh |
| a cough | **kašlja** | kahsh·lyah |
| diarrhea | **proljeva** | proh·lyeh·vah |
| a headache | **glavobolje** | glah·voh·boh·lyeh |
| insect bites | **uboda insekata** | oo·boh·dah ihn·seh·kah·teh |
| motion [travel] | **mučnine od vožnje** | |
| sickness | | mooch·nih·neh ohd vohzh·nyeh |
| a sore throat | **grlobolje** | gr·loh·boh·lyeh |
| sunburn | **opeklina od sunca** | oh·peh·klih·nah ohd soon·tsah |
| a toothache | **zubobolje** | zoo·boh·boh·lyeh |
| an upset stomach | **pokvarenog želuca** | poh·kvah·reh·nohg zheh·loo·tsah |

## YOU MAY SEE…

| | |
|---|---|
| **JEDNOM/TRI PUTA DNEVNO** | once/three times a day |
| **TABLA** | tablets |
| **KAP** | drop |
| **ČAJNA ŽLICA** | teaspoon |
| **POSLIJE/PRIJE JELA** | after/before meals |
| **UZ JELO** | with meals |
| **NA TAŠTE** | on an empty stomach |
| **GUTATI CIJELO** | swallow whole |
| **MOŽE UZROKOVATI POSPANOST** | may cause drowsiness |
| **SAMO ZA VANJSKU UPORABU** | for external use only |

## Basic Supplies

I'd like… **Htio** *m*/**Htjela** *f* **bih…** htih·oh/htyeh·lah bih…

acetaminophen [paracetamol]
**paracetamol** pah·rah·tseh·tah·mohl

aftershave **losion poslije brijanja**
oh·sih·ohn pohs·lih·yeh brih·yah·nyah

antiseptic cream **antiseptičnu kremu** ahn·tih·seh·ptih·chnoo kreh·moo

aspirin **aspirin** ah·spih·rihn

bandages **zavoj** zah·vohy

a comb **češalj** cheh·shahly

condoms **prezervative** preh·zehr·vah·tih·veh

contact lens solution
**otopinu za kontaktne leće**
oh·toh·pih·noo zah kohn·tahk·tneh leh·cheh

deodorant **dezodorans** deh·zoh·doh·rahns

a hairbrush **četku za kosu** cheh·tkoo zah koh·soo

ibuprofen **brufen** broo·fehn

insect repellent **sredstvo protiv insekata**
srehd·stvoh proh·tihv ihn·seh·kah·tah

| a nail file | **turpija/rašpa za nokte** |
| | *toor·pee·yah/rah·shpah zah noh·kteh* |
| a (disposable) | **brijač (za jednokratnu uporabu)** |
| razor | *brih·yahch (zah yeh·dnoh·krah·tnoo oo·poh·rah·boo)* |
| razor blades | **britvice** *brih·tvih·tseh* |
| sanitary napkins | **higijenske uloške** |
| [pads] | *hih·gih·yehn·skeh oo·loh·shkeh* |
| a scissors | **škare** *shkah·re* |
| shampoo/ | **šampon/regenerator** |
| conditioner | *shahm·pohn/reh·geh·neh·rah·tohr* |
| soap | **sapun** *sah·poon* |
| sunscreen | **kremu za sunčanje** |
| | *kreh·moo zah soon·chah·nyeh* |
| tampons | **tampone** *tahm·poh·neh* |
| tissues | **maramice** *mah·rah·mih·tseh* |
| toilet paper | **toaletni papir** *toh·ah·leh·tnih pah·pihr* |
| a toothbrush | **četkicu za zube** |
| | *cheh·tkih·tsoo zah zoo·beh* |
| toothpaste | **pastu za zube** |
| | *pah·stoo zah zoo·beh* |

For Baby Essentials, see page 144.

## The Basics

### Grammar

#### Regular Verbs

In Croatian, infinitives end in **ti** or **ći**. There are four different conjugation patterns of regular verbs. In the following pages are the present, past and future forms of the verbs **imati (to have)**, **ići (to go)**, **raditi (to work)**, **putovati (to travel)**. Each represents one conjugation pattern.

| IMATI (to have) | | Present | Past | Future |
| --- | --- | --- | --- | --- |
| I | **ja** | imam | sam imao m /imala f | ću imati |
| you (sing.) | **ti** | imaš | si imao m /imala f | ćeš imati |
| he/she/it | **on** m/ **ona** f/**ono** | ima | je imao m /imala f/imalo | će imati |
| we | **mi** | imamo | smo imali m /imale f | ćemo imati |
| you (pl./fml.) | **vi/Vi** | imate | ste imali | ćete imati |
| they | **oni** m/ **one** f/**ona** | imaju | su imali m/ imale f/imala | će imati |

| IĆI (to go) | | Present | Past | Future |
| --- | --- | --- | --- | --- |
| I | **ja** | idem | sam išao m /išla f | ću ići |
| you (sing.) | **ti** | ideš | si išao m /išla f | ćeš ići |
| he/she/it | **on** m/ **ona** f/**ono** | ide | je išao m /išla f/išlo | će ići |
| we | **mi** | idemo | smo išli | ćemo ići |

| | | | | |
|---|---|---|---|---|
| you (pl./fml.) | vi/Vi | idete | ste išli | ćete ići |
| they | oni m/ one f/ona | idu | su išli m/ išle f/išla | će ići |

| RADITI (to work) | | Present | Past | Future |
|---|---|---|---|---|
| I | ja | radim | sam radio m /radila f | ću raditi |
| you (sing.) | ti | radiš | si radio m/ radila f | ćeš raditi |
| he/she/it | on m/ ona f/ono | radi | je radio m/ radila f/radilo | će raditi |
| we | mi | radimo | smo radili | ćemo raditi |
| you (pl./fml.) | vi/Vi | radite | ste radili | ćete raditi |
| they | oni m/ one f/ona | rade | su radili m/ radile f/radila | će raditi |

| PUTOVATI (to travel) | | Present | Past | Future |
|---|---|---|---|---|
| I | ja | putujem | sam putovao m /putovala f | ću putovati |
| you (sing.) | ti | putuješ | si putovao m /putovala f | ćeš putovati |
| he/she/it | on m/ ona f/ono | putuje | je putovao m/ putovala f/putovalo | će putovati |
| we | mi | putujemo | smo putovali | ćemo putovati |
| you (pl./fml.) | vi/Vi | putujete | ste putovali | ćete putovati |
| they | oni m/ one f/ona | putuju | su putovali m/ putovale f/ putovala | će putovati |

## Irregular Verbs

There are only two irregular verbs in Croatian: **biti (to be)** and **htjeti (to want)**. The verb **biti** is used as the auxiliary verb to form the past tense.

| BITI | | Present | Past | Future |
|------|------|---------|------|--------|
| I | ja | sam | sam bio m/ bila f | ću biti |
| you (sing.) | ti | si | si bio m/bila f | ćeš biti |
| he/she/it | on m/ ona f/ono | je | je bio m/bila f/ bilo | će biti |
| we | mi | smo | smo bili | ćemo biti |
| you (pl./fml.) | vi/Vi | ste | ste bili | ćete biti |
| they | oni m/ one f/ona | su | su bili m/bile f/ bila | će biti |

The short form of the verb **htjeti** (indicated in parentheses in the table below) is used to build the future tense.

| HTJETI | | Present | Past | Future |
|--------|------|---------|------|--------|
| I | ja | hoću (ću) | sam htio m/ htjela f | ću htjeti |
| you (sing.) | ti | hoćeš (ćeš) | si htio m/ htjela f | ćeš htjeti |
| he/she/it | on m/ ona f/ono | hoće (će) | je htio m/ htjela f/htjelo | će htjeti |
| we | mi | hoćemo (ćemo) | smo htjeli | ćemo htjeti |
| you (pl./fml.) | vi/Vi | hoćete (ćete) | ste htjeli | ćete htjeti |
| they | oni m/ one f/ona | hoće (će) | su htjeli m/ htjele f/htjela | će htjeti |

# Imperatives

Imperatives are formed by adding the appropriate ending to the stem of the verb.

Example: Walk!

| you (sing./infml.) | **Hodaj!** |
| we | **Hodajmo!** |
| you (pl./fml.) | **Hodajte!** |

# Nouns

Nouns in Croatian can be masculine, feminine or neuter. Masculine nouns usually end in a consonant, feminine nouns usually end in **a**, and neuter nouns in **o** or **e**. There are no articles in Croatian; instead, when necessary, the words **jedan** *m*/**jedna** *f*/**jedno (one)** and **taj** *m*/**ta** *f*/**to (this)** are used.

Nouns in Croatian decline; that is, the noun's ending changes to reflect case. There are seven cases: **nominative, genitive, dative, accusative, instrumental, locative** and **vocative.**

In the **nominative** (subject) case, the plural is usually formed by adding **i** to masculine nouns, **e** to feminine nouns and **a** to neuter nouns.

# Word Order

In Croatian, the word order is usually as in English: **subject verb object**. If the subject is a personal pronoun, it is omitted; the verb ending indicates person and number. A personal pronoun is included only for emphasis.

Example:

**(Ja) Radim u Zagrebu.** I work in Zagreb.

**Radi li on u Zagrebu? Ne, ja radim u Zagrebu.**

Does he work in Zagreb? No, I work in Zagreb.

To ask a question, reverse the order of the subject and verb and add the word **li** between them or add the words **da li** before them. These two ways of asking questions are interchangeable. When using key question words such as **kada** (when) the words **da li** and **li** are not used.

Examples:

**Putujete u Split?** Do you travel to Split?
**Da li putujete u Split?** Do you travel to Split?
**Kada putujete u Split?** When do you travel to Split?

## Negation

To form a **negative sentence**, add **ne (not)** before a verb.

Examples:

**Pijemo vino.** We drink wine.
**Ne pijemo vino.** We don't drink wine.
**Ne** is always written separately, except in three verbs, which have irregular negatives: **biti (to be), htjeti (to want)** and **imati (to have).**

|  |  | BITI | HTJETI | IMATI |
|---|---|---|---|---|
| I | **ja** | **nisam** | **neću** | **nemam** |
| you (sing.) | **ti** | **nisi** | **nećeš** | **nemaš** |
| he/she/it | **on** m/ **ona** f/**ono** | **nije** | **neće** | **nema** |
| we | **mi** | **nismo** | **nećemo** | **nemamo** |
| you (pl./fml.) | **vi/Vi** | **niste** | **nećete** | **nemate** |
| they | **oni** m/ **one** f/**ona** | **nisu** | **neće** | **nemaju** |

In Croatian, the negative is also used with **nikad** (never), **nitko** (nobody) and **ništa** (nothing).

Example: **Nikad ne gledam TV.** I never watch TV.

## Pronouns

Pronouns are declined by case. The following list includes pronouns in the nominative (subject) case.

| I | **ja** |
| you (sing./infml.) | **ti** |
| he | **on** |
| she | **ona** |
| it | **ono** |
| we | **mi** |
| you (pl.) | **vi** |
| you (fml.) | **Vi** |
| they | **oni** *m*/**one** *f*/**ona** |

There are two forms for "you" in Croatian. The informal forms **ti** (singular) or **vi** (plural) are used when talking to friends, relatives and among young people. The **Vi** (polite/plural) form is used when speaking to one or more persons in a formal setting.

## Adjectives

**Adjectives** describe nouns and must agree with the nouns in gender, number and case. In Croatian, adjectives usually come before the noun. In the nominative case, **masculine adjectives** generally end with a consonant, **feminine adjectives** usually end in **a** and **neuter adjectives** in **o**.

Examples:

**Vaš sin je lijep.** Your son is nice.

**Vaša kćerka je lijepa.** Your daughter is nice.

**Ovaj plavi cvijet je krasan.** This blue flower is beautiful.

## Comparative & Superlative

**The comparative**, meaning "more", is usually formed by adding gender-specific suffixes. The superlative is formed by adding the prefix **naj** to the comparative form.

The **comparative**, meaning "less", is formed by adding the word **manje** (less) before the adjective.

Example:

|  | big | bigger | the biggest |
|---|---|---|---|
| masculine | **velik** | **veći** | **najveći** |
| feminine | **velika** | **veća** | **najveća** |
| neuter | **veliko** | **veće** | **najveće** |

|  | expensive | less expensive | least expensive |
|---|---|---|---|
| masculine | **skup** | **manje skup** | **najmanje skup** |
| feminine | **skupa** | **manje skupa** | **najmanje skupa** |
| neuter | **skupo** | **manje skupo** | **najmanje skupo** |

## Adverbs & Adverbial Expressions

**Adverbs** are used to describe verbs. Some adverbs are formed by adding **o** to the adjective.

The following are some common adverbial time expressions:

**trenutno** presently
**još ne** not yet
**još** still
**više ne** not anymore

# Numbers

## ESSENTIAL

| | |
|---|---|
| 0 | **nula** *noo·lah* |
| 1 | **jedan** *yeh·dahn* |
| 2 | **dva** *dvah* |
| 3 | **tri** *trih* |
| 4 | **četiri** *cheh·tih·rih* |
| 5 | **pet** *peht* |
| 6 | **šest** *shehst* |
| 7 | **sedam** *seh·dahm* |
| 8 | **osam** *oh·sahm* |
| 9 | **devet** *deh·veht* |
| 10 | **deset** *deh·seht* |
| 11 | **jedanaest** *yeh·dah·nah·ehst* |
| 12 | **dvanaest** *dvah·nah·ehst* |
| 13 | **trinaest** *trih·nah·ehst* |
| 14 | **četrnaest** *cheh·tr·nah·ehst* |
| 15 | **petnaest** *peh·tnah·ehst* |
| 16 | **šestnaest** *sheh·snah·ehst* |
| 17 | **sedamnaest** *seh·dahm·nah·ehst* |
| 18 | **osamnaest** *oh·sahm·nah·ehst* |
| 19 | **devetnaest** *deh·veht·nah·ehst* |
| 20 | **dvadeset** *dvah·deh·seht* |
| 21 | **dvadeset** jedan *dvah·deh·seht yeh·dahn* |
| 22 | **dvadeset** dva *dvah·deh·seht dvah* |
| 30 | **trideset** *trih·deh·seht* |
| 31 | **trideset jedan** *trih·deh·seht yeh·dahn* |
| 40 | **četrdeset** *cheh·tr·deh·seht* |

| 50 | **pedeset** peh·deh·seht |
| 60 | **šestdeset** shehst·deh·seht |
| 70 | **sedamdeset** seh·dahm·deh·seht |
| 80 | **osamdeset** oh·sahm·deh·seht |
| 90 | **devetdeset** deh·veh·deh·seht |
| 100 | **sto** stoh |
| 101 | **sto jedan** stoh yeh·dahn |
| 200 | **dvjesto** dvyeh·stoh |
| 500 | **petsto** peht·stoh |
| 1,000 | **tisuću** tih·soo·choo |
| 10,000 | **deset tisuća** deh·seht tih·soo·chah |
| 1,000,000 | **milijun** mih·lih·yoon |

## Ordinal Numbers

| first | **prvi** pr·vih |
| second | **drugi** droo·gih |
| third | **treći** treh·chih |
| fourth | **četvrti** cheh·tvr·tih |
| fifth | **peti** peh·tih |
| once | **jednom** yeh·dnohm |
| twice | **dvaput** dvah·poot |
| three times | **tri puta** trih poo·tah |

## Time

**ESSENTIAL**

| What time is it? | **Koliko je sati?** koh·lih·koh yeh sah·tih |
| It's noon [midday]. | **Podne je.** poh·dneh yeh |
| At midnight. | **U ponoć.** oo poh·nohch |

| | |
|---|---|
| From one o'clock to two o'clock. | **Od jedan do dva sata.** *ohd yeh·dahn doh dvah sah·tah* |
| Five after [past] three. | **Tri i pet.** *trih ih peht* |
| A quarter to four. | **Petnaest do četiri.** *peht·nah·ehst doh cheh·tih·rih* |
| 5:30 a.m./p.m. | **peti trideset/sedamnaesti trideset** *peh·tih trih·deh·seht/seh·dahm·nah·ehs·tih trih·deh·seht* |

Croatians use the 24-hour clock when writing time, especially in schedules. The morning hours from 1:00 a.m. to noon are the same as in English. After that, just add 12 to the time: so 1:00 p.m. would be 13:00, and 5:00 p.m. would be 17:00, and so on.

## Days

### ESSENTIAL

| | |
|---|---|
| Monday | **ponedjeljak** *poh·neh·dyeh·lyahk* |
| Tuesday | **utorak** *oo·toh·rahk* |
| Wednesday | **srijeda** *srih·yeh·dah* |
| Thursday | **četvrtak** *cheh·tvr·tahk* |
| Friday | **petak** *peh·tahk* |
| Saturday | **subota** *soo·boh·tah* |
| Sunday | **nedjelja** *neh·dyeh·lyah* |

## Dates

| | | |
|---|---|---|
| yesterday | **jučer** | *yoo·chehr* |
| today | **danas** | *dah·nahs* |
| tomorrow | **sutra** | *soo·trah* |
| day | **dan** | *dahn* |
| week | **tjedan** | *tyeh·dahn* |
| month | **mjesec** | *myeh·sehts* |
| year | **godina** | *goh·dih·nah* |

## Months

| | | |
|---|---|---|
| January | **sječanj** | *syeh·chahny* |
| February | **veljača** | *veh·lyah·chah* |
| March | **ožujak** | *oh·zhoo·yahk* |
| April | **travanj** | *trah·vahny* |
| May | **svibanj** | *svih·bahny* |
| June | **lipanj** | *lih·pahny* |
| July | **srpanj** | *sr·pahny* |
| August | **kolovoz** | *koh·loh·vohz* |
| September | **rujan** | *roo·yahn* |
| October | **listopad** | *lih·stoh·pahd* |
| November | **studeni** | *stoo·deh·nih* |
| December | **prosinac** | *proh·sih·nahts* |

## Seasons

| | | |
|---|---|---|
| spring | **proljeće** | *proh·lyeh·cheh* |
| summer | **ljeto** | *lyeh·toh* |
| fall [autumn] | **jesen** | *yeh·sehn* |
| winter | **zima** | *zih·mah* |

## Holidays

| | | |
|---|---|---|
| January 1: | New Year's Day | **Nova Godina** |
| January 6: | Epiphany | **Sveta tri kralja** |
| May 1: | Labor Day | **Praznik rada** |
| June 22: | Day of Antifascist Struggle | **Dan antifašističke borbe** |
| June 25: | Statehood Day | **Dan državnosti** |
| August 15: | Homeland Thanksgiving Day | **Dan domovinske zahvalnosti** |
| October 8: | Independence Day | **Dan neovisnosti** |
| November 1: | All Saint's Day | **Svi sveti** |
| December 25: | Christmas | **Božić** |

## Conversion Tables

### Mileage

| | |
|---|---|
| **1 km** – 0.62 mi | **20 km** – 12.4 mi |
| **5 km** – 3.10 mi | **50 km** – 31.0 mi |
| **10 km** – 6.20 mi | **100 km** – 61.0 mi |

### Measurement

| | | |
|---|---|---|
| 1 gram | **gram** *grahm* | = 0.035 oz. |
| 1 kilogram (kg) | **kilo** *kee·loh* | = 2.2 lb |
| 1 liter (l) | **litr** *leetr* | = 1.06 U.S./0.88 Brit. quarts |
| 1 centimeter (cm) | **centymetr** *tsehn·tyh·mehtr* | = 0.4 inch |
| 1 meter (m) | **metr** *mehtr* | = 3.28 feet |
| 1 kilometer (km) | **kilometr** *kee·loh·mehtr* | = 0.62 mile |

## Temperature

| | | |
|---|---|---|
| -40° C | – | -40° F |
| -30° C | – | -22° F |
| -20° C | – | -4° F |
| -10° C | – | 14° F |
| -5° C | – | 23° F |
| -1° C | – | 30° F |
| 0° C | – | 32° F |
| 5° C | – | 41° F |
| 10° C | – | 50° F |
| 15° C | – | 59° F |
| 20° C | – | 68° F |
| 25° C | – | 77° F |
| 30° C | – | 86° F |
| 35° C | – | 95° F |

## Oven Temperature

| | | | | | |
|---|---|---|---|---|---|
| 100° C | – | 212° F | 177° C | – | 350° F |
| 121° C | – | 250° F | 204° C | – | 400° F |
| 149° C | – | 300° F | 260° C | – | 500° F |

# Dictionary

ored
e
r
tska
odvijač

...a

...aurant riblji restoran
... morska bolest
...et sezonska karta
... mjesto
...tion (train) rezen...

challe...
shampo...
share v (ros...
sharp oštar
shaving brush četk...
shaving cream krema za ...
she ona
sheet (bed) plahta
shirt košulja
shock (electric) ud...
shoe cipela
shoe repair po...
shoe store p...
shop assist...
shopping
shoppi...

## A

**a little** malo
**a lot** puno
**a.m. prije** podne
**about** o
**abroad** inozemstvo
**accept** v prihvatiti
**access** pristup
**accident (road)** nezgoda
**accidentally** slučajno
**accountant** računovođa
**acne** akna
**across** preko
**acrylic** adj akrilni; n akrilik
**actor** glumac
**actress** glumica
**adapter** adapter
**address** adresa
**admission charge** ulaznica
**adult** n odrasla osoba
**afraid** uplašen
**after (time)** poslije; (place) iza
**afternoon** poslijepodne
**aftershave** losion poslije brijanja
**after-sun lotion** losion poslije **sunčanja**
**ago** prije
**agree, to** složiti se
**air conditioner** klima-uređaj
**air conditioning** klimatizacija
**air mattress** dušek na puhanje
**airline** zračna kompanija
**airmail** zračna pošta
**airport** zračna luka

**air-sickness bag** vrećica za povraćanje
**aisle seat** sjedište kraj prolaza
**alarm clock** budilica
**alcoholic** alkoholni
**allergic** alergičan
**allergy** alergija
**allowance** dozvola
**almost** skoro
**alone** sam
**already** već
**also** također
**alter** popraviti
**aluminum foil** aluminijska folija
**always** uvijek
**amazing** divan
**ambassador** ambasador
**ambulance** hitna pomoć
**American** adj američki; n Amerikanac
**amount** (money) iznos
**and** i
**anesthesia** anestezija
**animal** životinja
**another** drugi
**antibiotics** antibiotik
**antique** antika
**antiseptic** antiseptik
**antiseptic cream** antiseptična krema
**any** ikakav
**anyone** itko
**apartment** stan
**apologize** ispričati se
**appetite** tek
**appetizer** predjelo

| **adj** adjective | **BE** British English | **prep** preposition |
| **adv** adverb | **n** noun | **v** verb |

**appointment** (business) sastanak; (doctor) zakazana posjeta
**approximately** oko
**area code** pozivni broj
**arm (body part)** ruka
**around (time, place)** oko
**arrive** (car, train) stići; (plane) sletjeti
**art gallery** umjetnička galerija
**artist** umjetnik
**ashtray** pepeljara
**ask** (question) pitati; (request) tražiti
**aspirin** aspirin
**asthma** astma
**at** (time, place) u
**at least** barem
**ATM** bankomat
**attack** *n* napad
**attraction** (monument) znamenitost
**attractive** privlačan
**audio guide** audio-vodič
**Australia** Australija
**authenticity** autentičnost
**automatic** transmission automatski mjenjač
**autumn** [BE] jesen
**available** (free) slobodan
**avalanche** lavina

## B

**baby** beba
**baby bottle** bočica za bebe
**baby food** dječja hrana
**baby wipe** maramice za bebe
**babysitter** dadilja
**back** (body part) leđa
**backache** bol u leđima
**backpack** *n* ruksak; *v* putovati s ruksakom
**bad** loš
**bag** torba
**baggage** [BE] prtljaga

**bakery** pekarnica
**balcony** balkon
**ball** lopta
**ballet** balet
**band** (musical group) grupa
**bandage** zavoj
**bank** banka
**bar** bar
**barbecue** roštilj
**barber** brijačnica
**basement** podrum
**basketball** košarka
**bathroom** kupaonica
**bathtub** kada
**battery** baterija; (car) akumulator
**battleground** borilište
**be** biti
**beach** plaža
**beam** (headlights) svjetlo
**beard** brada
**beautiful** prekrasan
**because** jer
**bed** krevet
**bed and breakfast** polupansion
**bedding** prostirka
**bedroom** spavaća soba
**before** (time) prije
**begin** početi
**beginner** početnik
**behind** iza
**belong** pripadati
**belt** remen
**berth** (on ship) brodska kabina; (on train) ležaj
**best** najbolji
**bet** *v* kladiti se
**better** bolji
**between** između
**bib** siperak

**bicycle** bicikl
**big** velik
**bigger** veći
**bikini** bikini
**bill** (restaurant) račun
**binoculars** dvogled
**bird** ptica
**birthday** rođendan
**bite** *n* ugriz
**bitter** gorak
**bizarre** čudan
**bladder** mjehur
**bland** blijed
**blanket** deka
**bleach** izbjeljivač
**bleed** krvariti
**bleeding** krvarenje
**blind** slijep
**blister** žulj
**block** *v* blokirati
**blood** krv
**blood group** krvna grupa
**blood pressure** krvni tlak
**blouse** bluza
**blow-dry** feniranje
**board, to; embark** ukrcati (se)
**boarding card** karta za ukrcavanje
**boat trip** putovanje brodom
**boil** (ailment) čir; *v* (food) obariti; (water) kuhati
**boiler** bojler
**bone** kost
**book** knjiga
**bookstore** knjižara
**boot** *n* čizma
**boring** dosadan
**born** rođen
**borrow** posuditi
**botanical garden** botanički vrt

**bother** dosađivati
**bottle** boca
**bottle opener** otvarač za boce
**bowl** zdjela
**box** (container) kutija
**boxing** boks
**boy** dječak
**boyfriend** dečko
**bra** grudnjak
**bracelet** narukvica
**brake** kočnica
**break** (destroy) pokvariti; (a body part) slomiti
**break down, to** pokvariti (se)
**breakdown truck** [BE] vučna služba
**breakfast** doručak
**breast** (body part) grudi
**breastfeed** dojiti
**breathe** disati
**bridge** most
**briefs** (clothing) gaćice
**bring** donijeti
**Britain** Britanija
**British** *adj* britanski; *n* Britanac
**brochure** brošura
**broken** slomljen
**bronchitis** bronhitis
**brooch** broš
**broom** metla
**brother** brat
**browse** (shop) razgledati
**bruise** modrica
**bucket** kanta
**bug** (insect) buba
**build** graditi
**building** zgrada
**burn** goriti
**bus** autobus
**bus route** autobusna linija

**bus station** (for long-distance buses) autobusni kolodvor
**bus stop** autobusna postaja
**business** posao
**business center** poslovni centar
**business class** biznis klasa
**business hours** radno vrijeme
**businessman** poslovan čovjek
**busy** zauzet
**but** ali
**butane** gas butan
**butcher** (store) mesnica
**button** dugme
**buy** kupiti
**by** (place) kod; (time) do

**C**

**cabaret** kabare
**cafe** kafić
**call** (telephone) telefonirati
**camera** fotoaparat
**camera case** futrola za fotoaparat
**camp** *v* kampirati
**campfire** logorska vatra
**campsite** kamp
**can** *n* konzerva
**can opener** otvarač za konzerve
**Canada** Kanada
**canal** kanal
**cancel** poništiti
**cancer** (disease) rak
**cap** (dental) zubna kapica; (clothing) kapa
**car** automobil; (train) vagon
**car hire** [BE] rent-a-car
**car insurance** osiguranje vozila
**car park** [BE] parkiralište
**car rental** rent-a-car
**car seat** sjedalo
**carafe** vrč

**caravan** kamp-kućica
**card** karta
**careful** pažljiv
**carpet** (rug) tepih
**cart** kolica
**carton** paket
**cash** (money) gotovina; *v* platiti
**cashier** kasa
**casino** kasino
**castle** dvorac
**catch** (bus) uhvatiti
**cathedral** *katedrala*
**cave** špilja
**CD** CD
**CD player** CD-player
**cell phone** mobilni telefon
**cemetery** groblje
**ceramics** keramika
**certificate** potvrda
**chain** lanac
**change** *n* (money) promijeniti; (small coins) razmijeniti; (in shop) zamijeniti; *v* (bus, train) presjedati; (baby) presvući
**charcoal** drveni ugljen
**charge** naplata
**charter flight** čarter let
**cheap** jeftin
**check** *n* ček
**check book** čekovna knjižica
**check in** *n* registracija putnika
**check out** (hotel) odjaviti (se)
**check-in desk** šalter za registriranje
**cheers** (toast) živjeli
**chemical toilet** kemijski zahod
**chemist** [BE] ljekarna
**cheque** [BE] ček
**cheque book** [BE] čekovna knjižica
**chess** šah
**chest** (body) prsa

**child** dijete
**child's seat** dječija sjedalica
**children** djeca
**church** crkva
**cigar** cigara
**claim check** zahtjev za odštetu
**clamp** lisice
**clean** *adj* čist; *v* čistiti
**cleaning supply** sredstvo za čišćenje
**cliff** greben
**cling film** [BE] prozirna kuhinjska folija
**clinic** klinika
**clock** sat
**close** (near) blizu; *v* zatvoren
**clothing store** prodavaonica odjeće
**cloudy** oblačan
**club** (golf) palica za golf
**coach** [BE] (long-distance bus) autobus
**coat** kaput
**coat check** garderoba
**coat hanger** vješalica
**cockroach** žohar
**code** (area, dialing) pozivni broj
**coin** kovanica
**cold** *adj* (weather) hladno; *n* hunjavica
**collapse** klonuti
**collect** skupiti
**collect call** poziv na račun
    primatelja poziva
**color** boja
**color film** film u boji
**comb** češalj
**come** doći
**commission** provizija
**company** (business) poduzeće;
    (companionship) društvo
**composer** skladatelj
**computer** računar
**concert** koncert

**concert hall** koncertna dvorana
**concession** koncesija
**concussion** potres (mozga)
**conditioner** regenerator
**condom** prezervativ
**conductor** dirigent
**confirm** potvrditi
**confirmation** potvrda
**connect** (internet) konektirati
**connection** (train) veza
**conscious** svjestan
**constant** konstantan
**constipation** začepljenje
**consulate** konzulat
**consult** konzultirati se
**contact** kontaktirati
**contact lens** kontaktna leća
**contagious** zarazan
**contain** sadržati
**contemporary dance** suvremeni ples
**contraceptive** kontracepcijski
**convention hall** kongresna sala
**cook** *n* kuhar; *v* kuhati
**cooker** [BE] štednjak
**cooking** (cuisine) kuhinja
**cooking facilities** mogućnost kuhanja
**copper** bakar
**copy** kopirati
**corkscrew** vadičep
**correct** ispravan
**cosmetics** kozmetički proizvodi
**cost** *v* koštati
**cot** kolijevka
**cottage** koliba
**cotton** (material) pamuk
**cough** *n* kašalj; *v* kašljati
**country** (state) država
**country code** državni pozivni broj
**country music** country glazba

**course** (meal) način ishrane; (medication) terapija; (track, path) pravac kretanja
**cousin** rođak
**craft** shop obrt
**cramp** grč
**credit card** kreditna kartica
**credit card** number broj kreditne kartice
**crib** dječiji krevetić
**Croatia** Hrvatska
**Croatian** adj hrvatski; n Hrvat
**cross** v (street) prijeći
**crowd** gužva
**crown** (dental) zubna kruna; (royal) kruna
**cruise** n krstarenje
**crutches** štake
**crystal** (quartz) kristal
**cup** šalica
**cupboard** plakar
**currency** valuta
**currency exchange office** mijenjačnica
**currency exchange rate** tečaj mijenjanja novca
**curtain** zastor
**customs** carina
**customs declaration** carinska prijava
**cut glass** kristal
**cut** v (hair) šišati; (wound) posjeći
**cycle route** biciklistička staza
**cycling** biciklizam

## D

**daily** adj svakodnevni; adv svakodnevno
**damaged** oštećen
**damp** para
**dance club** disko klub
**dance** n ples; v plesati
**dangerous** opasan
**dark** taman

**daughter** kćerka
**dawn** zora
**day** dan
**day ticket** dnevna karta
**dead** (battery) prazna
**deaf** gluh
**deck chair** ležaljka
**declare** prijaviti
**deduct** odbiti
**deep** dubok
**defrost** odmrznuti
**degree (temperature)** stupanj
**delay** kašnjenje
**delayed** sa zakašnjenjem
**delicatessen** delikatesna radnja
**delicious** ukusan
**deliver** dostaviti
**delivery** dostava
**denim** traper
**dental** floss zubni konac
**dentist** zubar
**denture** zubna proteza
**deodorant** dezodorans
**depart** (train, bus) polazak
**department store** robna ruća
**departure lounge** čekaonica
**departures** (airport) polasci
**deposit** (safety) kaucija
**describe** opisati
**description** opis
**destination** (travel) odredište
**detail** detalj
**detergent** deterdžent
**develop** (photos) izraditi
**diabetes** dijabetes
**diabetic** n dijabetičar
**dialing code** pozivni broj
**diamond** dijamant
**diaper** pelena

**diarrhea** proljev
**dice kocka** za igru
**dictionary** rječnik
**diesel** dizel
**diet** dijeta
**difficult** težak
**dining car** vagon-restoran
**dining room** blagovaonica
**dinner** večera
**direct** *adj* (train, journey) direktni; *v* (to a place) uputiti
**direction** pravac
**director** (company) ravnatelj
**directory** (telephone) imenik
**dirty** prljav
**disabled** nepokretan
**discount** popust
**discount card** karta za popust
**dish** (meal) jelo
**dishcloth** kuhinjska krpa
**dishwasher** perilica za posuđe
**dishwashing liquid** sredstvo za pranje posuđa
**dislocated** premješten
**display cabinet** oglasna ploča
**display case** vitrina (izlog)
**disposable camera** jednokratni fotoaparat
**disturb** ometati
**dive** roniti
**diving equipment** ronilačka oprema
**divorced** rastavljen
**dizziness** vrtoglavica
**do** raditi
**doctor** liječnik
**dog** pas
**doll** lutka
**dollar** (U.S.) dolar
**domestic** (flight) domaći

**door** vrata
**double bed** bračni krevet
**double room** dvokrevetna soba
**downtown area** centar grada
**dress** haljina
**drink** *n* piće; *v* piti
**drink menu** karta pića
**drive** voziti
**driver** (car) vozač
**driver's license** vozačka dozvola
**drop** *n* kap
**drown** utopiti (se)
**drunk** pijan
**dry clean** *v* kemijski čistiti
**dry cleaner** kemijska čistionica
**dubbed** (movie) sinkroniziran
**during** tijekom
**duty** carina
**duvet** pokrivač

## E

**ear** uho
**ear drops** kapi za uho
**earache** bol u uhu
**earlier** ranije
**early** *adj* rani; *adv* rano
**earring** naušnica
**east** istok
**easy** lako
**eat** jesti
**economy class** ekonomska klasa
**elastic** *adj* elastičan
**electric shaver** električni brijač
**electrical outlet** električna utičnica
**electronic** elektronski
**electronic game** elektronska igra
**elevator** lift
**e-mail address** e-mail adresa
**e-mail** *n* e-mail; *v* poslati e-mail
**embassy** ambasada

**embroidery** ručni vez
**emerald** smaragd
**emergency** hitan slučaj
**emergency exit** izlaz u slučaju opasnosti
**emergency ward** intenzivna njega
**empty** prazan
**enamel** emajl
**end** n kraj; v završiti
**engaged** zaručen
**engine** (machine) stroj; (train) lokomotiva
**engineer** inženjer
**engineering** inženjerstvo
**England** Engleska
**English** adj engleski; n Englez
**engrave** urezati
**enjoy** uživati
**enjoyable** prijatan
**enlarge** (photos) uvećati
**enough** dosta
**entertainment guide** program zabavnih događanja
**entrance fee** cijena ulaznice
**envelope** kuverta
**epilepsy** padavica
**epileptic** n epileptičar
**equipment** (sports) oprema
**era** era
**error** greška
**escalator** pokretne stepenice
**essential** glavni
**e-ticket** e-karta
**European Union** (E.U.) Europska Zajednica (E.Z.)
**evening** večer
**evening dress** večernja haljina
**every** svaki
**every day** svaki dan
**every hour** svaki sat

**examination** (medical) pregled
**example** primjer
**except** osim
**excess luggage** višak prtljage
**exchange** zamijeniti
**exchange rate** tečaj
**excursion** izlet
**exhausted** iscrpljen
**exit** izlaz
**expensive** skup
**experienced** iskusan
**expiration date** rok trajanja
**expiry date** [BE] rok trajanja
**exposure** (photos) snimak
**express** ekspres
**express mail** brza pošta
**extension** (phone) priključak
**external** vanjski
**extra** (additional) dodatni
**extract** (tooth) vaditi
**eye** oko

**F**
**fabric** materijal
**face** lice
**factor** (sun) faktor
**faint** v klonuti
**fairground** luna-park
**fall** n jesen
**family** obitelj
**family name** prezime
**famous** slavan
**fan** (electric) ventilator; (folding) lepeza
**far** daleki
**farm** farma
**far-sighted** dalekovidan
**fast** brzo
**fast-food** fast food
**fat free** bez masnoće
**father** otac

**faucet** slavina
**faulty** pokvaren
**favorite** omiljeni
**fax** faks
**fax machine** faks-uređaj
**fee** naknada
**feed** nahraniti
**feel** osjećati (se)
**female** ženski
**ferry** trajekt
**fever** vrućica
**few** nekolicina
**fiancé** zaručnik
**fiancée** zaručnica
**field** polje
**fight** *n* svađa
**fill out** (form) popuniti
**fill up** (car) napuniti do vrha
**filling** (dental) plomba
**film** (camera, movie) film
**find** naći
**fine** (penalty) kazna; (well) dobar
**finger** prst
**fire** vatra
**fire alarm** požarni alarm
**fire brigade** [BE] vatrogasci
**fire department** vatrogasci
**fire door** požarni izlaz
**fire extinguisher** aparat za gašenje
  požara
**firewood** drvo za ogrjev
**first class** prva klasa
**first name** ime
**fish store** ribarnica
**fit** pristajati
**fitting room** kabina za presvlačenje
**fix** *v* popraviti
**flame** plamen
**flashlight** džepna lampa

**flavor** okus
**flight** let
**flight number** broj leta
**flip-flops** japanke
**floor** (level) kat
**florist** cvjećarnica
**flower** cvijet
**flu** gripa
**flush** vodokotlić
**fly** *n* (insect) muha; *v* letjeti
**fog** magla
**folk art** narodna umjetnost
**folk music** narodna muzika
**follow** (pursue) pratiti; (road, sign) slijediti
**food** hrana
**foot** stopalo
**football** [BE] nogomet
**for** (time) za
**foreign currency** strana valuta
**forest** šuma
**forget** zaboraviti
**fork** vilica
**form** *n* (document) obrazac
**formal dress** službeno odijelo
**fortunately** na sreću
**fountain** vodoskok
**foyer** (hotel, theater) foaje
**fracture** lom
**frame** (glasses) okvir
**free** (available) slobodan; (without
  charge) besplatan
**freezer** zamrzivač
**frequently** često
**fresh** svjež
**friend** prijatelj
**friendly** (person) ljubazan; (place,
  atmosphere) ugodan
**frightened** preplašen
**from** od

**front** (face) čelo
**frost** mraz
**frying** pan tava
**full** pun
**full board** puni pansion
**full-service** potpuna usluga
**fun** zabava
**funny** smiješan
**furniture** namještaj
**fuse** osigurač
**fuse box** kutija sa osiguračima

## G

**game** n (play) igra; (sports) utakmica
**garage** (mechanic) automehaničarska radnja; (parking lot) parking garaža
**garbage** smeće
**garbage bags** vrećice za smeće
**garden** vrt
**gas** (fuel) gorivo
**gas station** benzinska postaja
**gate** (airport) izlaz
**gay club** gay klub
**genuine** pravi
**get** (buy) kupiti; (find) naći
**get back** (return) vratiti (se)
**get off** (bus, train) sići
**get to** doći do
**gift** poklon
**gift shop** darovni dućan
**gift wrap** pakiranje darova
**girl** djevojka
**girlfriend** djevojka
**give** dati
**gland** žlijezda
**glass** čaša
**glasses** (optical) naočale
**glove** rukavica
**go** ići
**go away** odlaziti

**go on** nastaviti
**go shopping** ići u nabavku
**go to** (travel to) ići u
**goggles** (swimming) naočale za plivanje; (skiing) zaštitne naočale
**gold** zlato
**gold plated** pozlaćen
**golf** golf
**golf course** teren za golf
**good** dobar
**good day** dobar dan
**good evening** dobra večer
**good morning** dobro jutro
**good night** laku noć
**goodbye** doviđenja
**gram** gram
**grandfather** djed
**grandmother** baka
**grass** trava
**graze** n ogrebotina
**great** adj velik; adv izvrsno
**grocery store**
  [BE] trgovina mješovite robe
**ground** (earth) zemlja
**ground floor** prizemlje
**groundcloth** podloga za šator
**groundsheet** [BE] prostirka
**group** grupa
**group leader** vođa grupe
**guarantee** n garancija
**guest** gost
**guesthouse** gostionica
**guide** (tour) vodič
**guidebook** vodič
**guided tour** tura s vodičem
**guitar** gitara
**gym** teretana
**gynecologist** ginekolog

## H

**hair** kosa
**hair foam** pjena za kosu
**hair gel** gel za kosu
**haircut** šišanje
**hairspray** lak za kosu
**hairstylist** frizer
**halal** halal
**half** pola
**hammer** čekić
**hand** ruka
**hand luggage** [BE] ručna prtljaga
**handbag** [BE] torbica
**handicapped** hedikepiran
**handicrafts** rukotvorine
**hanger** vješalica
**happen** dogoditi se
**happy** sretan
**harbor** luka
**hard** (difficult) težak
**hat** šešir
**have** imati
**head** *n* glava; *v* (go towards) voditi
**headache** glavobolja
**health** zdravlje
**health food store**
    trgovaonica zdrave hrane
**health insurance**
    zdravstveno osiguranje
**hear** čuti
**hearing aid** slušni aparat
**heart** srce
**heart attack** srčani udar
**heat** grijanje
**heater** radijator
**heating** [BE] grijanje
**heavy** težak
**height** visina
**helmet** kaciga

**help** pomoć
**hemorrhoids** hemoroidi
**her** njen
**here** ovdje
**hers** njen
**high** visok
**highchair** stolica za hranjenje djece
**highlight** *n* (hair) pramenovi; *v* (stress)
    naglasiti
**highway** autoput
**hiking** (general) pješačenje; (trip)
    stopiranje
**hill** brijeg
**him** njemu
**hire** *v* unajmiti
**his** njegov
**historic site** povjesno mjesto
**hobby** (pastime) hobi
**hold on** (wait) čekati
**holiday** [BE] odmor
**home** (be, go) dom
**honeymoon** medeni mjesec
**horse** konj
**horse racing** konjska utrka
**hospital** bolnica
**hot** vruć
**hot spring** izvor vruće vode
**hot water** vruća voda
**hotel** hotel
**hour** sat
**house** kuća
**hug** *v* zagrliti
**hungry** gladan
**hurt** boliti
**husband** muž

## I

**icy** leden
**identification** osobna isprava
**ill** [BE] bolestan

**illegal** ilegalan
**imitation** imitacija
**imported** uvozni
**in** (place) u; (period of time) za
**included** uračunat
**incredible** nevjerovatan
**indicate** ukazati
**indigestion** slabo varenje
**indoor pool** zatvoreni bazen
**inexpensive** jeftin
**infected** zaražen
**infection** infekcija
**inflammation** upala
**informal** (dress) neslužben
**information** (desk, office) informacije
**injection** injekcija
**injured** ozlijeđen
**innocent** nevin
**insect** insekt
**insect bite** ubod insekta
**insect repellent** odbojan za insekte
**inside** unutra
**insist** nastojati
**insomnia** nesanica
**instead** umjesto
**instruction** uputa
**instructor** instruktor
**insulin** inzulin
**insurance** osiguranje
**insurance card** kartica osiguranja
**insurance claim**
    potraživanje od osiguranja
**interest** (hobby) zanimanje
**interested** zainteresiran
**interesting** zanimljiv
**international** (flight) međunarodni
**International Student Card**
    Međunarodna Studentska Iskaznica
**internet** internet

**internet cafe** internet cafe
**interpreter** prevoditelj
**intersection** raskrižje
**into** u
**intolerance** netolerancija
**introduce oneself** predstaviti se
**invite** pozvati
**iodine** jod
**Ireland** Irska
**iron** *n* željezo
**island** otok
**itch** svrbiti
**item** (object) predmet
**itemized bill** detaljan račun

**J**

**jacket** jakna
**jaw** čeljust
**jazz** jazz
**jeans** traperice
**jellyfish** meduza
**jet-lag** jet-lag
**jet-ski** jet ski
**jeweler** zlatarnica
**jewelry** nakit
**join** (a group) pridružiti se
**joint** (body) zglob
**joke** šala
**journalist** novinar
**journey** putovanje
**jumper** [BE] džemer
**junction** [BE] (intersection) raskrižje

**K**

**keep** čuvati
**kerosene** prečišćeni petrolej
**kettle** čajnik
**key** ključ
**key card** (hotel) kartica od sobe
**kiddie pool** gumeni bazen
**kidney** bubreg

**kilometer** kilometar
**kind** *adj* drag; *n* vrsta
**kiss** *n* poljubac; *v* poljubiti
**kitchen** kuhinja
**kitchen foil** [BE] aluminijska folija
**knee** koljeno
**knife** nož
**know** znati
**kosher** košer

**L**

**label** (sticker) etiketa; (on bottle) naljepnica
**lace** čipka
**ladder** ljestve
**lake** jezero
**lamp** lampa
**land** *v* sletjeti
**language course** *tečaj jezika*
**large** velik
**last** *adj* (previous) zadnji; *v* trajati
**late** (not early) kasni; (delayed) sa zakašnjenjem
**later** *adv* kasnije
**launderette** [BE] praonica
**laundromat** praonica
**laundry** facilities mogućnost pranja veša
**lavatory** umivaonik
**lavender** lavanda
**lawyer** odvjetnik
**laxative** laksativ
**lead** *n* (material) olovo; *v* voditi
**leak** *n* procjep; *v* (roof, pipe) curiti
**learn** (language) učiti
**leather** koža
**leave** (depart) odlaziti; (deposit) ostaviti; (go) ići; (depart of plane) polijetati
**left** *adj* lijevi
**leg** noga
**legal** legalan

**lend** posuditi
**length** (piece) dužina
**lens** (optical) leća; (camera) objektiv
**lens cap** poklopac za objektiv
**less** manje
**lesson** lekcija
**let go** pustiti
**let** *v* (permit) dozvoliti
**letter** pismo
**level** *adj* ravan
**library** knjižnica
**license plate** number registracijska oznaka auta
**life boat** čamac za spašavanje
**life jacket** prsluk za spašavanje
**life preserver** kolut za spašavanje
**lifeguard** spasavalac
**lift** [BE] (elevator) lift
**lift pass** (skiing) skipass
**light** *adj* (weight) lagan; (color) svjetal; *n* svjetlo
**lightbulb** žarulja
**lighter** *n* upaljač
**like** *v* sviđati se
**limousine** limuzina
**linen** lan
**lip** usna
**lipgloss** sjajilo za usne
**lipstick** ruž za usne
**liquor store** prodavaonica pića
**liter** litar
**little (small)** mali
**live** u živo
**live music** glazba u živo
**liver** jetra
**living room** dnevna soba
**loafers** mokasinke
**lobby** (theater) foaje; (hotel) predsoblje
**local** lokalni

**lock** *n* (door) ključaonica; (bike) lanac; *v* zaključati
**log on** logirati
**log off** odlogirati
**login** login
**long** dugačak
**long-distance** bus autobus
**long-sighted** [BE] dalekovidan
**look** *v* gledati
**look for** tražiti
**loose** širok
**lorry** [BE] kamion
**lose (wallet)** izgubiti
**lost-and-found** izgubljeno i pronađeno
**loud** glasan
**love** *n* ljubav; *v* voljeti
**lovely** dražesno
**low** nizak
**lower** (berth) donji
**luck** sreća
**luggage** prtljaga
**luggage cart** kolica za prtljagu
**luggage locker** pretinac za prtljagu
**luggage trolley** [BE] kolica za prtljagu
**lump** čvoruga
**lunch** ručak
**lung** pluća

## M

**machine washable** prati u perilici
**madam** gospođa
**magazine** časopis
**magnificent** predivan
**mail** *n* pošta; *v* slati poštu
**mailbox** poštanski sandučić
**main** glavni
**main street** glavna ulica
**make** napraviti
**male** muški
**man** muškarac

**manager** upravitelj
**manicure** manikura
**manual** transmission ručni mjenjač
**many** mnogo
**map** zemljopisna karta
**market** (job market) tržište; (marketplace) tržnica
**married** (male) oženjen; (female) udana
**mascara** maskara
**mask** (diving) maska
**mass** masa
**massage** masaža
**match** *n* (light) šibica; (play) utakmica
**mattress** dušek
**maybe** možda
**meal** ručak
**measure** mjera
**measurement** mjerenje
**measuring cup** šalica za mjerenje
**measuring spoon** žlica za mjerenje
**mechanic** mahanički
**medication** lijek
**medicine** liječenje
**medium** srednji
**meet** (get to know) upoznati; (appointment) sresti
**meeting room** prostorija za sastanke
**member** (association) član
**memorial** (war) spomenik
**memory card** memorijska kartica
**men** (restroom) muški
**mention** spomenuti
**menu** meni
**message** poruka
**metal** metal
**microwave** *(oven)* mikrovalna pećnica
**midday** [BE] podne
**midnight** ponoć
**migraine** migrena

**mine** moj
**mini-bar** mini-bar
**minute (time) minuta**
**mirror** zrcalo
**miss** (lack) propustiti; (lose) izgubiti
**mistake** pogreška
**misunderstanding** nesporazum
**mobile home** kamp-kućica
**mobile phone** [BE] mobilni telefon
**moisturizer** (cream) hidrantna krema
**moment** trenutak
**monastery** samostan
**money** novac
**money order** novčana uputnica
**month** mjesec
**monument** spomenik
**mop krpa** za pod
**moped** moped
**more** više
**morning** (a.m.) jutro; (time) ujutro
**mosque** džamija
**mosquito** bite ubod komarca
**mother** majka
**motion sickness** mučnina od vožnje
**motorboat** motorni čamac
**motorcycle** motor
**motorway** [BE] autoput
**mountain** planina
**mountain bike** mountain bike
**mountain pass** planinski prolaz
**mountain range** planinski vijenac
**moustache** brkovi
**mouth** usta
**move** v (change of room) preseliti
**movie** film
**movie theater** kino
**much** mnogo
**mug** v napasti
**mugging** napad

**muscle** mišić
**museum** muzej
**music** glazba
**music store** glazbena prodavaonica
**musician** glazbenik
**must** v morati
**my** moj

# N

**nail file** turpija za nokte
**nail salon** kozmetički salon
**name** ime
**name** day imendan
**napkin** ubrus
**nappy** [BE] pelena
**narrow** uzak
**national** narodni
**national park** nacionalni park
**nationality** narodnost
**native** izvorni
**nature reserve** park prirode
**nausea** mučnina
**near** blizak
**nearby** ublizini
**nearest** najbliži
**near-sighted** kratkovidan
**necessary nužan**
**neck** (clothing) okovratnik; (body) vrat
**necklace** ogrlica
**need** v trebati
**nephew** (sister's son) sestrić; (brother's son) bratić
**nerve** živac
**nervous system** nervni sustav
**never** nikad
**new** novi
**New Year** Nova Godina
**New Zealand** Novi Zeland
**newsagent** [BE] kiosk
**newspaper** novine

**newsstand** kiosk
**next** sljedeći
**nice** lijep
**niece** (sister's daughter) sestrićna; (brother's daughter) bratićna
**night** noć
**nighttime surcharge** noćna tarifa
**no** ne
**no one** nitko
**noisy** bučan
**non-alcoholic** bezalkoholan
**none** nijedan
**nonsense** besmisao
**non-smoker** nepušač
**non-smoking** *adj* nepušački
**noon** podne
**normal** normalan
**north** sjever
**nose** nos
**not bad** nije loše
**nothing** ništa
**notify** obavijestiti
**now** sada
**number** broj
**nurse** medicinska sestra
**nylon** najlon

**O**

**occasionally** povremeno
**occupied** zauzet
**odds** (betting) šansa
**of course** naravno
**office** (place) ured
**off-licence** [BE] prodavaonica pića
**off-peak** izvan prometnih sati
**often** često
**oil** ulje
**old** star
**old town** stari grad
**on** u

**on business** poslovno
**on foot** pješice
**once** jednom
**one-way** jednosmjeran
**one-way ticket** jednosmjerna karta
**open** *adj* otvoren; *v* otvoriti
**opening hours** radno vrijeme
**opera** opera
**opera house** opera
**operation** operacija
**opposite** nasuprot
**optician** optičar
**or** (either/ or) ili
**order** *n* (restaurant) narudžba; *v* naručiti
**our(s)** naš
**outdoor** na otvorenom
**outdoor pool** otvoreni bazen
**outrageous** pretjeran
**outside** vani
**oval** ovalan
**oven** pećnica
**overcharge** *v* preračunati se
**overheat** pregrijati
**overlook** vidikovac
**overnight** preko noći
**owe** dugovati
**own** *adj* vlastiti
**owner** vlasnik

**P**

**p.m.** poslije podne
**pacifier** duda
**pack** (oneself) pakirati (se)
**package** paket
**paddling pool** [BE] gumeni bazen
**pail** (toy) kantica
**pain** bol
**painkiller** sredstvo protiv bolova
**paint** slikati
**painter** slikar

**painting** slika
**pair** par
**pajamas** pidžama
**palace** palača
**palpitation** lupanje srca
**panorama** panorama
**pants** hlače
**pantyhose** hulahopke
**paper towel** papirnati ubrus
**paralysis** paraliza
**parents** roditelji
**park** n park; v parkirati
**parking garage** parking garaža
**parking lot** parkiralište
**parking meter** automat na parkiralištu
**parliament building** zgrada parlamenta
**partner** (romance, business) partner
**party** (social) stranka
**pass** (place) prolaz
**passenger** putnik
**passport** putovnica
**passport number** broj putovnice
**password** lozinka
**pastry shop** slastičarnica
**patch** n flaster
**patient** n pacijent
**pavement** [BE] pločnik
**pay** platiti
**pay phone** javni telefon
**peak** vrh
**pearl** perla
**pebbly** (beach) kamenit
**pedestrian** pješački
**pedestrian crossing** pješački prelaz
**pedestrian precinct** [BE] pješačka zona
**pedestrian zone** pješačka zona
**pen** olovka
**people** ljudi
**per** po

**perhaps** možda
**period** (menstrual) mjesečnica; (time) razdoblje
**person** osoba
**petrol** [BE] gorivo
**petrol station** [BE] benzinska postaja
**pewter** kositar
**pharmacy** ljekarna
**phone card** telefonska kartica
**phone** n telefon; v telefonirati
**photo** fotografija
**photocopier** stroj za fotokopiranje
**photograph** fotografirati
**photographer** fotograf
**phrase** izraz
**phrase book** jezični priručnik
**pick up** podići
**picnic** piknik
**picnic area** područje za piknik
**piece** (item) dio; (amount) komad
**pill** (contraceptive) pilula; (tablet) tableta
**pillow** jastuk
**pillow case** jastučnica
**pipe** (smoking) lula; (water, gas) cijev
**pitch** (camping) podići šator
**pizzeria** pizzeria
**place** mjesto
**plan** n plan; v planirati
**plane** ravan
**plant** (greenery) biljka
**plaster** [BE] (adhesive bandage) flaster
**plastic** adj plastičan
**plastic bag** plastična vrećica
**plastic wrap** prozirna kuhinjska folija
**plate** tanjur
**platform** peron
**platinum** platina
**play** n (theater) predstava; v igrati
**playground** igralište

**playwright** dramski pisac
**pleasant** prijatan
**please** v zamoliti
**pleasure** zadovoljstvo
**plug** utičnica
**plunger** odčepljivač odvoda
**pneumonia** upala pluća
**point** točka
**poison** otrov
**police** policija
**police report** policijski izvještaj
**police station** policijska postaja
**polyester** poliester
**pond** ribnjak
**pop** (music) pop glazba
**popular** (well-known) poznati
**port** (harbor) luka
**porter** nosilac
**portion** porcija
**possible** moguć
**post** n (mail) pošta; v poslati
**post office** pošta
**post stamp** poštanska markica
**postage** poštarina
**postbox** [BE] poštanski sandučić
**postcard** razglednica
**poster** plakat
**pot** (for cooking) lonac; (for tea) čajnik
**pottery** lončarstvo
**pound** (sterling) funta britanska
**powdery** (snow) praškast
**power** (electricity) električna struja
**power cut** nestanak struje
**precipice** litica
**pregnant** trudna
**prepaid phone card** nadoplatni bon
za telefon
**prescribe** propisati
**prescription** liječnički recept

**press** n tisak; v glačati
**pretty** zgodan
**price** cijena
**print** n tisak; v ispisati
**prison** zatvor
**produce store** trgovina mješovite robe
**profession** zanimanje
**program** program
**pronounce** izgovoriti
**pub** pub
**public** n javnost
**pump** (gas station) pumpa
**puncture** procjep
**puppet show** lutkarska predstava
**pure** čist
**purse** torbica
**push-chair** [BE] dječija kolica
**put** staviti
**pyjamas** [BE] pidžama

**Q**

**quality** kakvoća
**quarter** (place) četvrt; (time) petnaest
**queue** [BE] v čekati u redu
**quick** brz
**quickly** brzo
**quiet** tih

**R**

**race course** [BE] hipodrom
**racetrack** hipodrom
**racket** (tennis, squash) reket
**railway station** [BE] željeznički kolodvor
**rain** n kiša
**raincoat** kišni mantil
**rape** n silovanje; v silovati
**rapids** brzaci
**rare** (unusual) rijadak
**rash** n osip
**razor** brijač
**razor blade** britvica

**read** *v* čitati
**ready** spreman
**real** (genuine) pravi
**rear lights** zadnja svjetla
**receipt** račun
**receive** dobiti
**reception** (desk) recepcija
**receptionist** recepcionar
**recommend** preporučiti
**recycling** reciklaža
**reduction** (price) sniženje
**refrigerator** hladnjak
**refund** povrat novca
**region** (area) područje
**registered mail** preporučena pošta
**registration form** *prijavnica*
**reliable** pouzdan
**religion** vjera
**remember** sjećati se
**rent** iznajmiti
**rental car** iznajmljeni automobil
**repair** *n* popravak; *v* popraviti
**repeat** ponoviti
**replacement** *n* zamjena
**replacement part** zamjenski dio
**report** (crime) prijaviti
**require** zahtijevati
**reservation** rezervacija
**reserve** *v* rezervirati
**rest** *v* odmoriti se
**restaurant** restoran
**return** (restore) vratiti
**return ticket** [BE] povratna karta
**returnable bottle** povratna boca
**reverse-charge call** [BE] poziv na račun primatelja poziva
**revolting** odbijajući
**rheumatism** reuma
**rib** rebro

**right** (correct) točan; (good) u redu
**right of way** prvenstvo prolaza
**ring** prsten
**river** rijeka
**road** cesta
**road map** autokarta
**road sign** prometni znak
**rob** opljačkati
**robbery** pljačka
**rock** (land formation) stijena; (music) rock glazba
**romantic** romaničan
**roof** (house, car) krov
**roof-rack** krovni spremnik za prtljagu
**room** (hotel) soba
**room service** posluga
**rope** konop
**round** okrugao
**round-trip ticket** povratna karta
**route** putanja
**rowboat** čamac na vesla
**rowing** veslanje
**rubbish** [BE] (trash) smeće
**rude** nepristojan
**ruins** ruševine
**run out** (fuel) ostati bez goriva
**rush** žurba
**rush hour** prometni sat

## S

**safe** *adj* siguran; *n* sef
**safety** sigurnost
**safety pin** ziherica
**sales tax** PDV
**sand** pijesak
**sandal** sandala
**sandy** (beach) pješčan
**sanitary napkin** higijenski uložak
**sanitary pad** [BE] higijenski uložak
**satellite TV** satelitska televizija

**satin** saten
**sauna** sauna
**say** *v* reći
**scarf** šal
**schedule** raspored
**scissors** škare
**scooter** skuter
**Scotland** Škotska
**screwdriver** odvijač
**sea** more
**sea front** riva
**seafood restaurant** riblji restoran
**seasickness** morska bolest
**season ticket** sezonska karta
**seat** (train) mjesto
**seat reservation** (train) rezervacija mjesta
**second class** druga klasa
**secretary** tajnik
**sedative** sedativ
**see** (observe, witness) vidjeti; (inspect) razgledati
**self-employed** samozaposlen
**self-service** (gas station) samoposluživanje
**sell** prodavati
**send** slati
**senior citizen** umirovljenik
**separated** razdvojen
**separately** odvojeno
**serious** ozbiljan
**service** (in restaurant) usluga; (religious) služba
**sex** seks; (gender) spol
**shade** sjena
**shady** taman
**shallow** plitak
**shampoo** šampon
**share** *v* (room) dijetiti

**sharp** oštar
**shaving brush** četka za brijanje
**shaving cream** krema za brijanje
**she** ona
**sheet** (bed) plahta
**shirt** košulja
**shock** (electric) udar
**shoe** cipela
**shoe repair** postolar
**shoe store** prodavaonica obuće
**shop assistant** prodavač
**shopping area** trgovački centar
**shopping basket** košara
**shopping centre** [BE] trgovački centar
**shopping mall** trgovački centar
**short** *adj* (not long) kratak
**shorts** (clothing) kratke hlače
**short-sighted** [BE] kratkovidan
**shoulder** rame
**shovel** (toy) lopatica
**show** *n* (presentation) priredba; (theater) predstava; *v* prikazati
**shower** tuš
**shrine** svetište
**shut** *adj* zatvoren; *v* zatvoriti
**shutter** (window) škura
**sick** bolestan
**side effect** nuspojava
**side order** prilog
**side street** bočna ulica
**sidewalk** pločnik
**sights** turističke atrakcije
**sightseeing tour** obilazak znamenitosti
**sign language** jezik znakova
**sign** *n* znak; *v* potpisati
**sign post** putokaz
**silk** svila
**silver** srebro
**singer** pjevač

**single** sam
**single room** jednokrevetna soba
**single ticket** jednosmjerna karta
**sink** sudoper
**sir** gospdin
**sister** sestra
**sit** sjesti
**size** veličina
**skewer** ražanj
**ski** skija
**ski boot** skijaška čizma
**ski pole** skijaški štap
**skin** koža
**skirt** suknja
**sleep** spavati
**sleeper wagon** [BE] spavaća kola
**sleeping bag** vreća za spavanje
**sleeping car** spavaća kola
**sleeping pill** tableta za spavanje
**sleeve** rukav
**slice** kriška
**slip** v kliziti
**slipper** kućna papuča
**slow** spor
**slowly** sporo
**small** mali
**smell** mirisati
**smoke** pušiti
**smoker** pušač
**smoking** (room) za pušače
**snack** zakuska
**snack bar** prezalogajnica
**sneaker** tenisica
**snorkel** dihalica
**snow** snijeg
**soap** sapun
**soccer** nogomet
**sock** čarapa
**sole** (shoes) đon

**soloist** solist
**some** neki
**something** nešto
**sometimes** nekad
**son** sin
**soon** uskoro
**soother** [BE] duda
**sore throat** grlobolja
**sorry** žalostan
**soul** (music) soul glazba
**sour** kisel
**south** jug
**souvenir** suvenir
**souvenir store** suvenirnica
**spa** spa
**space** prostor
**spare** rezervni
**speak** govoriti
**special** poseban
**specialist** specijalist
**specimen** proba
**spell** v sricati
**spend** (time) provesti; (money) trošiti
**spicy** začinjen
**sponge** spužva
**spoon** žlica
**sport** sport
**sporting goods store** prodavaonica sportske opreme
**spot** (place, site) mjesto
**sprained** uganut
**spring** proljeće
**square** (town) trg; (shape) kvadrat
**stadium** stadion
**staff** osoblje
**stain** mrlja
**stainless steel** nehrđajući čelik
**stairs** stepenice
**stamp** (postal) poštanska markica

**start** *v* (begin) početi, (car) upaliti
**starter** [BE] predjelo
**statement** (police) izjava
**statue** kip
**stay** *n* boravak; *v* (in a hotel) odsjesti
**sterilizing solution** sredstvo za desinfekciju
**still** *adv* još
**stolen** ukraden
**stomach** trbuh
**stomachache** bol u trbuhu
**stop** *n* (bus, tram) stanica; *v* zaustaviti (se)
**store** prodavaonica
**store directory** imenik
**storm** oluja
**stove** štednjak
**straight ahead** pravo naprijed
**strange** stran
**straw** (drinking) slamka
**stream** potok
**street** ulica
**stroller** dječija kolica
**strong** (potent) snažan
**student** student
**study** *v* studirati
**stunning** veličanstveno
**style** stil
**subtitled** s podtitlom
**suggest** predložiti
**suit** odijelo
**suitable** odgovarajući
**suitcase** kofer
**summer** ljeto
**sunbathe** sunčati se
**sunburn** opekline od sunca
**sunglasses** sunčane naočale
**sunny** sunčano
**sunscreen** krema za sunčanje
**sunstroke** sunčanica

**superb** super
**supermarket** supermarket
**supervision** nadzor
**supplement** dodatak
**sure** siguran
**surfboard** daska za surfanje
**surname** nadimak
**sweater** džemper
**sweet** (taste) sladak
**swelling** oticanje
**swim** plivati
**swimming** plivanje
**swimming pool** bazen
**swimming trunks** kupaće gaćice
**swimsuit** kupaći kostim
**swollen** napuhan
**symptom** (illness) simptom
**synagogue** sinagoga
**synthetic fiber** sintetičko vlakno

## T

**table** stol
**take** (carry) uzeti; (medicine) uzeti lijek; (time) trajati
**talk** razgovarati
**tall** visok
**tampon** tampon
**tan** ten
**tap** [BE] slavina
**tapestry** tapiserija
**taste** *v* kušati
**taxi** taksi
**taxi rank** [BE] taksi postaja
**taxi stand** taksi postaja
**teacher** učitelj
**team** ekipa
**teaspoon** čajna žlica
**teddy bear** medica
**telephone bill** telefonski račun
**telephone booth** telefonska govornica

**telephone call** telefonski poziv
**telephone** n telefon; v telefonirati
**telephone number** telefonski broj
**tell** reći
**temperature** (body) temperatura
**temple** hram
**temporarily** povremeno
**tennis** tenis
**tennis court** tenisko igralište
**tent** šator
**tent peg** klin za šator
**tent pole** šatorske štange
**terminal** terminal
**terrace** terasa
**terrible** grozan
**terrific** strašan
**text** n (phone) poruka
**thank** v zahvaliti se
**thank you** hvala
**that** taj
**theater** kazalište
**theft** krađa
**their(s)** njihov
**them** njima
**theme park** zabavni park
**then** (time) onda
**there** tamo
**thermometer** termometar
**thermos** termos-boca
**these** ti
**they** oni
**thick** debel
**thief** lopov
**thigh** uzak
**thin** tanak
**think** misliti
**thirsty** žedan
**this** (one) ovaj
**those** ti

**throat** grlo
**through** kroz
**thumb** palac
**ticket** karta
**ticket office** šalter za prodaju karata
**tie** n kravata
**tight** adv usko
**tights** [BE] (clothing) hulahopke
**time** vrijeme
**timetable** [BE] raspored
**tin opener** [BE] otvarač za konzerve
**tire** (car) guma
**tired** umoran
**tissue** maramica
**to** (place) u
**tobacco** duhan
**tobacconist** trafika
**today** danas
**toe** nožni prst
**toilet** zahod
**toilet paper** toaletni papir
**tomorrow** sutra
**tongue** (organ) jezik
**tonight** večeras
**tonsil** krajnik
**too** (extreme) previše
**tooth** zub
**toothache** zubobolja
**toothbrush** četkica za zube
**toothpaste** pasta za zube
**torn** razdvojen
**tour** izlet
**tour guide** vodič
**tourist** turist
**tourist office** turistički ured
**tow truck** vučna služba
**towel** ručnik
**tower** toranj
**town** grad

**town center** centar grada
**town hall** vječnica
**toy** igračka
**track** peron
**traditional** tradicionalni
**traffic** promet
**traffic jam** zastoj u prometu
**traffic light** semafor
**trailer** prikolica
**train** vlak
**train station** željeznički kolodvor
**tram** tramvaj
**transit** (travel) tranzit
**translate** prevesti
**translation** prijevod
**translator** tumač
**trash** smeće
**trash can** kanta za smeće
**travel** v putovati
**travel agency** putnička agencija
**travel sickness** [BE] mučnina od vožnje
**travelers check** putnički ček
**tree** drvo
**trim** v skratiti
**trip** putovanje
**trolley** [BE] kolica
**trousers** [BE] hlače
**truck** kamion
**true** istinit
**try** probati
**try on** (clothes) isprobati
**T-shirt** majica
**tumor** tumor
**tunnel** tunel
**turn** skrenuti
**turn down** (volume, heat) smanjiti
**turn off** ugasiti
**turn on** upaliti
**turn up** (volume, heat) pojačati

**TV** televizor
**tweezers** pinceta
**twist** v (hurt) uganuti
**type** (sort) vrsta
**typical** tipičan

## U

**ugly** ružan
**ulcer** čir
**umbrella** (rain) kišobran; (sun) suncobran
**uncle** (father's brother) stric; (mother's brother) ujak
**uncomfortable** neudoban
**unconscious** nesvjestan
**under** ispod
**underpants** [BE] gaćice
**understand** razumjeti
**undress** svući se
**uneven** (ground) neravan
**unfortunately** nažalost
**uniform** uniforma
**unit** (phone card) impuls
**United Kingdom** (U.K.) Ujedinjeno Kraljevstvo
**United States** (U.S.) S.A.D. (Sjedinjene Američke Države)
**university** sveučilište
**unleaded** bezolovni
**unlimited mileage** bez ograničenja kilometraže
**unlock** otključati
**unpleasant** neugodan
**unscrew** odvinuti
**urgent** hitan
**utensils** pribor za jelo

## V

**vacation** odmor
**vacuum cleaner** usisavač
**value** vrijednost

**VAT** [BE] PDV
**vegetarian** *n* vegetarijanac
**viewpoint** [BE] vidikovac
**vineyard** vinograd
**volleyball** odbojka

## W

**wait** čekati
**walk** *n* šetnja; *v* hodati
**wallet** novčanik
**warm** *v* zagrijati
**washing machine** perilica
**water** voda
**waterfall** vodopad
**weather forecast**
  vremenska prognoza
**week** tjedan
**weekend** vikend
**wheelchair ramp**
  ulaz za invalidska kolica

**where** gdje
**window** (house) prozor; (shop) izlog
**window seat** sjedalo do prozora
**wine list** vinska karta
**wireless** bežični
**wool** vuna
**work** *v* raditi

## X

**X-ray** rendgen

## Y

**yacht** jahta
**year** godina
**yes** da
**yesterday** jučer
**you** ti (sing.); vi (plural); Vi (formal)
**youth hostel** hostel

## Z

**zoo** zoološki vrt
**zero** nula

# A

**adapter** adapter
**adresa** address
**akna** acne
**akrilik** n acrylic
**akrilni** adj acrylic
**akumulator** battery (car)
**alergičan** allergic
**alergija** allergy
**ali** but
**alkoholni** alcoholic
**aluminijska folija**
  aluminum [kitchen BE] foil
**ambasada** embassy
**ambasador** ambassador
**američki** adj American
**Amerikanac** n American
**anestezija** anesthesia
**antibiotik** antibiotics
**antika** antique
**antiseptična krema** antiseptic cream
**antiseptik** antiseptic
**aparat za gašenje požara**
  fire extinguisher
**aspirin** aspirin
**astma** asthma
**audio-vodič** audio guide
**Australija** Australia
**autentičnost** authenticity
**autobus** bus
**autobusna linija** bus route
**autobusna postaja** bus stop
**autobusni kolodvor** bus station (for
  long-distance buses)
**autokarta** road map
**automat na parkiralištu**
  parking meter

**automatski mjenjač**
  automatic transmission
**automehaničarska radnja**
  garage (mechanic)
**automobil** car
**autoput** highway [motorway BE]

# B

**baka** grandmother
**bakar** copper
**balet** ballet
**balkon** balcony
**banka** bank
**bankomat** ATM
**bar** bar
**barem** at least
**baterija** battery
**bazen** swimming pool
**beba** baby
**benzinska postaja**
  gas [petrol BE] station
**besmisao** nonsense
**besplatan** free (without charge)
**bez kofeina** decaffeinated
**bez masnoće** fat free
**bez ograničenja kilometraže**
  unlimited mileage
**bezalkoholan** non-alcoholic
**bezolovni** unleaded
**bežični** wireless
**bicikl** bicycle
**biciklistička staza** cycle route
**biciklizam** cycling
**bikini** bikini
**biljka** plant (greenery)
**biti** be
**biznis klasa** business class
**blagovaonica** dining room

**blijed** bland
**blizak** near
**blokirati** *v* block
**bluza** blouse
**boca** bottle
**bočica za bebe** baby bottle
**bočna ulica** side street
**boja** color
**bojler** boiler
**boks** boxing
**bol** pain
**bol** *u* leđima backache
**bol u trbuhu** stomachache
**bol u uhu** earache
**bolestan** sick [ill BE]
**boliti** hurt
**bolnica** hospital
**bolji** better
**boravak** *n* stay
**borilište** battleground
**botanički vrt** botanical garden
**bračni krevet** double bed
**brada** beard
**brat** brother
**bratić** nephew (brother's son)
**brijač** razor
**brijačnica** barber
**brijeg** hill
**Britanac** *n* British
**Britanija** Britain
**britanski** *adj* British
**britvica** razor blade
**brkovi** moustache
**brodska kabina** berth (on ship)
**broj** number
**broj kreditne kartice** credit card
    *number*
**broj leta** flight number
**broj putovnice** passport number

**bronhitis** bronchitis
**broš** brooch
**brošura** brochure
**brz** quick
**brza pošta** express mail
**brzaci** rapids
**brzo** quickly
**buba** bug
**bubreg** kidney
**bučan** noisy
**budilica** alarm clock
**butan** butane gas

## C

**carina** duty (customs)
**carinska prijava** customs declaration
**CD** CD
**CD-player** CD player
**centar grada** downtown area
**cesta** road
**cigara** cigar
**cijena** price
**cijena ulaznice** entrance fee
**cijev** pipe (water, gas)
**cipela** shoe
**country glazba** country music
**crkva** church
**crven** red
**curiti** *v* leak (roof, pipe)
**cvijet** flower
**cvjećarnica** florist

## Č

**čajna žlica** teaspoon
**čajnik** kettle
**čamac na vesla** rowboat
**čamac za spašavanje** life boat
**čarapa** sock
**čarter let** charter flight
**časopis** magazine
**čaša glass**

**ček** *n* check [cheque BE]
**čekaonica** departure lounge
**čekati** wait
**čekić** hammer
**čekovna knjižica**
  check [cheque BE] book
**čelo** front (face)
**čeljust** jaw
**često** often
**češalj** comb
**četka za brijanje** shaving brush
**četkica za zube** toothbrush
**četvrt** quarter (place)
**čipka** lace
**čir** ulcer
**čist** *adj* clean
**čistiti** *v* clean
**čitati** *v* read
**čizma** *n* boot
**član** member (association)
**čudan** bizarre
**čuti** hear
**čuvati** keep
**čvoruga** lump

**D**

**dadilja** babysitter
**daleki** far
**dalekovidan**
  far-sighted [long-sighted BE]
**dan** day
**danas** today
**darovni dućan** gift shop
**daska za surfanje** surfboard
**dati** give
**debel** thick
**dečko** boyfriend
**deka** blanket
**delikatesna radnja** delicatessen
**detalj** detail

**detaljan račun** itemized bill
**deterdžent** detergent
**dezodorans** deodorant
**dihalica** snorkel
**dijabetes** diabetes
**dijabetičar** *n* diabetic
**dijamant** diamond
**dijeta** diet
**dijete** child
**dijetiti** *v* share (room)
**direktni** direct (train, journey)
**dirigent** conductor
**disati** breathe
**disko klub** dance club
**divan** amazing
**dizel** diesel
**djeca** children
**dječak** boy
**dječija hrana** baby food
**dječija kolica** stroller [push-chair BE]
**dječija sjedalica** child's seat
**dječiji krevetić** crib
**djed** grandfather
**djevojka** girlfriend
**dnevna karta** day ticket
**dnevna soba** living room
**do** by (time)
**dobar** good
**dobar dan** good day
**dobiti** receive
**dobra večer** good evening
**dobro jutro** good morning
**doći** come
**doći do** get to
**dodatak** supplement
**dodatni** extra (additional)
**dogoditi se** happen
**dojiti** breastfeed
**dolar** dollar (U.S.)

**dom** home, house
**domaći** domestic (flight)
**domaćica** housewife
**donijeti** bring
**donji** lower (berth)
**doručak** breakfast
**dosadan** boring
**dosađivati** bother
**dosta** enough
**dostava** delivery
**dostaviti** deliver
**doviđenja** goodbye
**dozvola** allowance
**dozvoliti** v let (permit)
**drag** adj kind
**dramski pisac** playwright
**dražesno** lovely
**druga klasa** second class
**drugi** another
**društvo** company (companionship)
**drveni ugljen** charcoal
**drvo** tree
**drvo za ogrjev** firewood
**država** country (state)
**državni pozivni broj** country code
**dubok** deep
**duda** pacifier [soother BE]
**dugačak** long
**dugme** button
**dugovati** owe
**duhan** tobacco
**dušek** mattress
**dušek na puhanje** air mattress
**dužina** length (piece)
**dvogled** binoculars
**dvokrevetna soba** double room
**dvorac** castle
**džamija** mosque
**džemper** sweater [jumper BE]

**džepna lampa** flashlight
**đon** sole (shoes)

## E

**e-karta** e-ticket
**ekipa** team
**ekonomska klasa** economy class
**ekspres** express
**elastičan** adj elastic
**električna struja** power (electricity)
**električna utičnica** electrical outlet
**električni brijač** electric shaver
**elektronska igra** electronic game
**elektronski** electronic
**e-mail** n e-mail
**e-mail adresa** e-mail address
**emajl** enamel
**Engleska** England
**engleski** adj English
**Englez** n English
**epileptičar** n epileptic
**era** era
**etiketa** label (sticker)
**Europska Zajednica (E.Z.)**
  European Union (E.U.)

## F

**faks** fax
**faks-uređaj** fax machine
**faktor** factor (sun)
**farma** farm
**fast food** fast-food
**feniranje** blow-dry
**film** film (camera, movie)
**film** u boji color film
**flaster** n patch [plaster BE]
**foaje** foyer (hotel, theater)
**fotoaparat** camera
**fotograf** photographer
**fotografija** photo
**fotografirati** photograph

**frizer** hairstylist
**funta** pound (sterling)
**futrola za fotoaparat** camera case

## G

**gaćice** briefs [underpants BE] (clothing)
**garancija** *n* guarantee
**garderoba** coat check
**gay klub** gay club
**gdje** where
**gel za kosu** hair gel
**ginekolog** gynecologist
**gitara** guitar
**glačati** *v* press
**gladan** hungry
**glasan** loud
**glava** head
**glavna ulica** main street
**glavni** main
**glavobolja** headache
**glazba** music
**glazba u živo** live music
**glazbena prodavaonica** music store
**glazbenik** musician
**gledati** *v* look
**gluh** deaf
**glumac** actor
**golf** golf
**gorak** bitter
**goriti** burn
**gorivo** gas [petrol BE] (fuel)
**gospdin** sir
**gospođa** madam
**gost** guest
**gostionica** guesthouse
**gotovina** cash (money)
**govoriti** speak
**grad** town
**graditi** build
**gram** gram

**grč** cramp
**greben** cliff
**greška** error
**grijanje** heat [heating BE]
**gripa** flu
**grlo** throat
**grlobolja** sore throat
**groblje** cemetery
**grozan** terrible
**grudi** breast (body part)
**grudnjak** bra
**grupa** group
**guma** tire (car)
**gumeni bazen** kiddie [paddling BE] pool
**gužva** crowd

## H

**haljina** dress
**hedikepiran** handicapped
**hemoroidi** hemorrhoids
**hidrantna krema** moisturizer (cream)
**higijenski uložak** sanitary napkin [pad BE]
**hipodrom** racetrack [race course BE]
**hitan** urgent
**hitan slučaj** emergency
**hitna pomoć** ambulance
**hlače** pants [trousers BE]
**hladan** *adj* cold
**hladno** *adv* cold
**hladnjak** refrigerator
**hobi** hobby (pastime)
**hodati** *v* walk
**hotel** hotel
**hram** temple
**hrana** food
**Hrvat** *n* Croatian
**Hrvatska** Croatia
**hrvatski** *adj* Croatian
**hulahopke**

pantyhose [tights BE] (clothing)
**hunjavica** *n* cold (illness)
**hvala** thank you

## I

**i** and
**ići** go
**ići u** nabavku go shopping
**igra** game (play)
**igračka** toy
**igralište** playground
**igrati (se)** *v* play
**ikakav** any
**ilegalan** illegal
**ili** or; either
**imati** have
**ime** name
**imendan** name day
**imenik** directory (telephone)
**imitacija** imitation
**impuls** unit (phone card)
**infekcija** infection
**informacije** information (desk, office)
**inozemstvo** abroad
**insekt** insect
**instruktor** instructor
**intenzivna njega** emergency ward
**internet** internet
**internet cafe** internet cafe
**inzulin** insulin
**inženjer** engineer
**inženjerstvo** engineering
**injekcija** injection
**Irska** Ireland
**iscrpljen** exhausted
**iskusan** experienced
**ispisati** *v* print
**ispod** under
**ispravan** correct
**ispričati se** apologize

**isprobati** try on (clothes)
**istinit** true
**istok** east
**itko** anyone
**iza** behind, after (place)
**izbjeljivač** bleach
**izgovoriti** pronounce
**izgubiti** lose (wallet)
**izjava** statement (police)
**izlaz** exit
**izlaz u slučaju opasnosti**
    emergency exit
**izlet** excursion
**izlog** window (shop)
**između** between
**iznajmiti** rent
**iznajmljeni automobil** rental car
**iznos** amount (money)
**izraditi** develop (photos)
**izraz** phrase
**izvan prometnih sati** off-peak
**izvor vruće vode** hot spring
**izvorni** native

## J

**jakna** jacket
**japanke** flip-flops
**jastučnica** pillow case
**jastuk** pillow
**javni telefon** pay phone
**javnost** *n* public
**jazz** jazz
**jednokratni fotoaparat**
    disposable camera
**jednokrevetna soba** single room
**jednom** once
**jednosmjeran** one-way
**jednosmjerna karta** one-way ticket
**jeftin** cheap
**jeftiniji** cheaper

**jelo** dish (meal)
**jer** because
**jesen** *n* fall [autumn BE]
**jesti** eat
**jet ski** jet-ski
**jet-lag** jet-lag
**jetra** liver
**jezero** lake
**jezični priručnik** phrase book
**jezik** tongue
**jezik znakova** sign language
**jod** iodine
**još** *adv* still
**jug** south
**jutro** morning (part of day)

## K

**kabare** cabaret
**kabina za presvlačenje** fitting room
**kaciga** helmet
**kada** bathtub
**kafić** cafe
**kakvoća** quality
**kamenit** pebbly (beach)
**kamion** truck [lorry BE]
**kamp** campsite
**kampirati** *v* camp
**kamp-kućica** caravan
**Kanada** Canada
**kanal** canal
**kanta** bucket
**kantica** pail (toy)
**kap** *n* drop
**kapa** cap (clothing)
**kapi za uho** ear drops
**kaput** coat
**karta** ticket
**karta pića** drink menu
**karta za popust** discount card
**karta za ukrcavanje** boarding card

**kartica** card
**kartica od sobe** key card (hotel)
**kartica osiguranja** insurance card
**kasa** cashier
**kasino** casino
**kasni** late (not early)
**kasnije** *adv* later
**kasniti** be late
**kašalj** *n* cough
**kašljati** *v* cough
**kašnjenje** delay
**kat** floor (level)
**katedrala** cathedral
**kaucija** deposit (security)
**kazalište** theater
**kazna** fine (penalty)
**kćerka** daughter
**kemijska čistionica** dry cleaner
**kemijski čistiti** dry-clean
**kemijski zahod** chemical toilet
**keramika** ceramics
**kilometar** kilometer
**kino movie** theater [cinema BE]
**kiosk** newsstand [newsagent BE]
**kip** statue
**kisel** sour
**kiša** *n* rain
**kišni mantil** raincoat
**kišobran** umbrella (rain)
**kladiti se** *v* bet
**klimatizacija** air conditioning
**klima-uređaj** air conditioner
**klin za šator** tent peg
**klinika** clinic
**klonuti** *v* faint
**ključ** key
**ključaonica** *n* lock (door)
**knjiga** book
**knjižara** bookstore

**knjižnica** library
**kocka za igru** dice
**kočnica** brake
**kod** by (place)
**kofer** suitcase
**kokice** popcorn
**koliba** cottage
**kolica** cart [trolley BE]
**kolica za prtljagu**
  luggage cart [trolley BE]
**kolijevka** cot
**koliko** how many, how much
**kolut za spašavanje** life preserver
**koljeno** knee
**komad** piece (amount)
**koncert** concert
**koncertna dvorana** concert hall
**koncesija** concession
**konektirati** connect (internet)
**kongresna sala** convention hall
**konop** rope
**konstantan** constant
**kontaktirati** contact
**kontaktna leća** contact lens
**kontracepcijski** contraceptive
**konzerva** *n* can
**konzulat** consulate
**konzultirati se** consult
**konj** horse
**konjska utrka** horse racing
**kopirati** copy
**kosa** hair
**kositar** pewter
**kost** bone
**košara** shopping basket
**košarka** basketball
**košer** kosher
**koštati** *v* cost
**košulja** shirt

**kovanica** coin
**kozmetički proizvodi** cosmetics
**kozmetički salon** nail salon
**koža** leather, skin
**krađa** theft
**kraj** *n* end
**krajnik** tonsil
**kratak** *adj* short (not long)
**kratke hlače** shorts (clothing)
**kratkovidan**
  near-sighted [short-sighted BE]
**kravata** *n* tie
**kreditna kartica** credit card
**krema za brijanje** shaving cream
**krema za sunčanje** sunscreen
**krevet** bed
**kristal** crystal (quartz)
**kriška** slice
**krov** roof (house, car)
**krovni spremnik za prtljagu** roof-rack
**kroz** through
**krpa za pod** mop
**krstarenje** *n* cruise
**kruna** crown (royal)
**krv** blood
**krvarenje** bleeding
**krvariti** bleed
**krvna grupa** blood group
**krvni tlak** blood pressure
**kuća** house
**kućna papuča** slipper
**kuhar** *n* cook
**kuhati** *v* cook
**kuhinja** kitchen
**kuhinjska krpa** dishcloth
**kupaće gaćice** swimming trunks
**kupaći kostim** swimsuit
**kupaonica** bathroom
**kupiti** buy

**kušati** *v* taste
**kutija** box (container)
**kutija sa osiguračima** fuse box
**kuverta** envelope
**kvadrat** square (shape)

## L

**lagan** *adj* light (weight)
**lak za kosu** hairspray
**lako** easy
**laksativ** laxative
**laku noć** good night
**lampa** lamp
**lan** linen
**lanac** *n* lock (bike)
**lavanda** lavender
**lavina** avalanche
**leća** lens (optical)
**leden** icy
**leđa** back (body)
**legalan** legal
**lekcija** lesson
**lepeza** fan (folding fan)
**let** flight
**letjeti** *v* fly
**ležaljka** deck chair
**lice** face
**lift** elevator [lift BE]
**liječenje** medicine
**liječnički recept** prescription
**liječnik** doctor
**lijek** medication
**lijep** nice
**lijevi** *adj* left
**limuzina** limousine
**lisice** clamp
**litar** liter
**litica** precipice
**login** login
**logirati** log on (internet)

**logorska vatra** campfire
**lokalni** local
**lokomotiva** engine (train)
**lom** fracture
**lonac** pot (for cooking)
**lončarstvo** pottery
**lopatica** shovel (toy)
**lopov** thief
**lopta** ball
**losion poslije brijanja** aftershave
**losion poslije sunčanja** after-sun lotion
**loš** bad
**lozinka** password
**luka** port (harbor)
**lula** pipe (smoking)
**luna-park** fairground
**lupanje srca** palpitation
**lutka** doll
**lutkarska predstava** puppet show
**ljekarna** pharmacy [chemist BE]
**ljestve** ladder
**ljeto** summer
**ljubav** *n* love
**ljubazan** friendly (person)
**ljudi** people

## M

**magla** fog
**mahanički** mechanic
**majica** T-shirt
**majka** mother
**mali** little (small)
**malo** a little
**manikura** manicure
**manje** less
**maramica** tissue
**maramice za bebe** baby wipe
**masa** mass
**masaža** massage
**maska** mask (diving)

**maskara** mascara
**materijal** fabric
**matirana izrada** matte finish (photo)
**medeni mjesec** honeymoon
**medicinska sestra** nurse
**meduza** jellyfish
**Međunarodna Studentska Iskaznica**
　　International Student Card
**međunarodni** international (flight)
**memorijska kartica** memory card
**meni** menu
**mesnica** butcher (store)
**metal** metal
**metla** broom
**migrena** migraine
**mijenjačnica** currency exchange office
**mikrovalna pećnica** microwave (oven)
**mini-bar** mini-bar
**minuta** minute (time)
**mirisati** smell
**misliti** think
**mišić** muscle
**mjehur** bladder
**mjera** measure
**mjerenje** measurement
**mjesec** month
**mjesečnica** period (menstrual)
**mjesto** *n* place (seat)
**mnogo** many, much
**mobilni telefon** cell [mobile BE] phone
**modrica** bruise
**moguć** possible
**mogućnost kuhanja** cooking facilities
**mogućnost pranja veša**
　　laundry facilities
**moj** my, mine
**mokasinke** loafers
**moped** moped
**morati** *v* must

**more** sea
**morska bolest** seasickness
**most** bridge
**motor** motorcycle
**motorni čamac** motorboat
**mountain bike** mountain bike
**možda** maybe
**mraz** frost
**mrlja** stain
**mučnina** nausea
**mučnina od vožnje**
　　motion [travel BE] sickness
**muha** fly (insect)
**muškarac** man
**muški** male
**muzej** museum
**muž** husband

# N

**na otvorenom** outdoor
**na sreću** fortunately
**nacionalni park** national park
**naći** get (find)
**nadimak** surname
**nadoplatni bon za telefon**
　　prepaid phone card
**nadzor** supervision
**naglasiti** *v* highlight (stress)
**nahraniti** feed
**najbliži** nearest
**najbolji** best
**najlon** nylon
**nakit** jewelry
**naknada** fee
**naljepnica** label (on bottle)
**namještaj** furniture
**naočale** glasses (optical)
**naočale za plivanje**
　　goggles (swimming)
**napad** *n* attack

**napasti** *v* mug
**naplata** charge
**napraviti** make
**napuhan** swollen
**napuniti do vrha** fill up (car)
**narančast** orange (color)
**naravno** of course
**narodna muzika** folk music
**narodna umjetnost** folk art
**narodni** national
**narodnost** nationality
**naručiti** *v* order
**narudžba** *n* order (restaurant)
**narukvica** bracelet
**nastaviti** go on
**nastojati** insist
**nasuprot** opposite
**naš** our(s)
**naušnica** earring
**nažalost** unfortunately
**ne** no
**nehrđajući čelik** stainless steel
**nekad** sometimes
**neki** some
**nekolicina** few
**nepokretan** disabled
**nepristojan** rude
**nepušač** non-smoker
**nepušački** *adj* non-smoking
**neravan** uneven (ground)
**nervni sustav** nervous system
**nesanica** insomnia
**neslužben** informal (dress)
**nesporazum** misunderstanding
**nestanak struje** power cut
**nesvjestan** unconscious
**nešto** something
**netolerancija** intolerance
**neudoban** uncomfortable

**neugodan** unpleasant
**nevin** innocent
**nevjerovatan** incredible
**nezgoda** accident (road)
**nije bitno** never mind
**nije loše** not bad
**nijedan** none
**nikad** never
**ništa** nothing
**nitko** no one
**nizak** low
**noć** night
**noćna tarifa** nighttime surcharge
**noga** leg
**nogomet** soccer [football BE]
**normalan** normal
**nos** nose
**nosilac** porter
**Nova Godina** New Year
**novac** money
**novčana uputnica** money order
**novčanik** wallet
**novi** new
**Novi Zeland** New Zealand
**novinar** journalist
**novine** newspaper
**nož** knife
**nožni prst** toe
**nuspojava** side effect
**nužan** necessary
**njegov** his
**njemu** him
**njen** her(s)
**njihov** their(s)
**njima** them

# O

**o** about
**obariti** *v* boil (food)
**obavijestiti** notify

**obilazak znamenitosti** sightseeing tour
**obitelj** family
**objektiv** lens (camera)
**oblačan** cloudy
**obrazac** *n* form (document)
**obrt** craft shop
**od** from
**odbijajući** revolting
**odbiti** deduct
**odbojan za insekte** insect repellent
**odbojka** volleyball
**odčepljivač odvoda** plunger
**odgovarajući** suitable
**odijelo** suit
**odjaviti (se)** check out (hotel)
**odlaziti** leave (depart)
**odlogirati** log off (internet)
**odmor** vacation [holiday BE]
**odmoriti se** *v* rest
**odmrznuti** defrost
**odrasla osoba** *n* adult
**odredište** destination (travel)
**odsjesti** stay (in a hotel)
**odvijač** screwdriver
**odvinuti** unscrew
**odvjetnik** lawyer
**odvojeno** separately
**oglasna ploča** display cabinet
**ogrebotina** *n* graze
**ogrlica** necklace
**ohlađen** chilled
**okej** OK
**oko** around (time, place); eye
**okovratnik** neck (clothing)
**okrugao** round
**okus** flavor
**okvir** frame (glasses)
**olovka** pen
**olovo** *n* lead (material)

**oluja** storm
**ometati** disturb
**omiljeni** favorite
**ona** she
**onda** then (time)
**oni** they
**opasan** dangerous
**opekline od sunca** sunburn
**opera** opera
**operacija** operation
**opis** description
**opisati** describe
**opljačkati** rob
**oprema** equipment (sports)
**optičar** optician
**osigurač** fuse
**osiguranje** insurance
**osiguranje vozila** car insurance
**osim** except
**osip** *n* rash
**osjećati (se)** feel
**osoba** person
**osoblje** staff
**osobna isprava** identification
**ostatak** *n* change (small coins)
**ostati bez goriva** run out (fuel)
**ostaviti** leave (deposit)
**oštar** sharp
**oštećen** damaged
**otac** father
**oticanje** swelling
**otključati** unlock
**otok** island
**otrov** poison
**otvarač za boce** bottle-opener
**otvarač za konzerve** can [tin BE] opener
**otvoren** *adj* open
**otvoreni bazen** outdoor pool
**otvoriti** *v* open

**ovaj** this (one)
**ovalan** oval
**ovamo** over here
**ovdje** here
**ozbiljan** serious
**ozlijeđen** injured
**oženjen** married

# P

**pacijent** *n* patient
**padavica** epilepsy
**paket** package
**pakiranje darova** gift wrap
**pakirati (se)** pack (oneself)
**palac** thumb
**palača** palace
**palica za golf** golf club
**pamuk** cotton (material)
**panorama** panorama
**papirnati ubrus** paper towel
**par** pair
**para** damp
**paracetamol acetaminophen**
   [paracetamol BE]
**paraliza** paralysis
**park** *n* park
**park prirode** nature reserve
**parking garaža** garage (parking lot)
**parking garaža** parking garage
**parkiralište** parking lot [car park BE]
**parkirati** *v* park
**partner** partner (romance, business)
**partnerka** partner (girlfriend)
**pas** dog
**pasta za zube** toothpaste
**pažljiv** careful
**PDV** sales tax [VAT BE]
**pećnica** oven
**pekarnica** bakery
**pelena** diaper [nappy BE]

**pepeljara** ashtray
**perilica** washing machine
**perilica za posuđe** dishwasher
**perla** pearl
**peron** track [platform BE]
**piće** *n* drink
**pidžama** pajamas
**pijan** drunk
**pijesak** sand
**piknik** picnic
**pilula** pill (contraceptive)
**pinceta** tweezers
**pismo** letter
**pitati** ask (question)
**piti** *v* drink
**pizzeria** pizzeria
**pjena za kosu** hair foam
**pješačenje** hiking (general)
**pješačka zona**
   pedestrian zone [precinct BE]
**pješački** pedestrian
**pješački prelaz** pedestrian crossing
**pješčan** sandy (beach)
**pješice** on foot
**pjevač** singer
**plahta** sheet (bed)
**plakar** cupboard
**plakat** poster
**plamen** flame
**plan** *n* plan
**planina** mountain
**planinski prolaz** mountain pass
**planinski vijenac** mountain range
**planirati** *v* plan
**plastičan** *adj* plastic
**plastična vrećica** plastic bag
**platina** platinum
**platiti** pay
**plaža** beach

**ples** *n* dance
**plesati** *v* dance
**plitak** shallow
**plivanje** swimming
**plivati** swim
**pločnik** sidewalk [pavement BE]
**plomba** filling (dental)
**pluća** lung
**pljačka** robbery
**po** per
**početi** begin
**početnik** beginner
**podići** pick up
**podići šator** pitch (camping)
**podloga za šator** groundcloth
**podne** noon [midday BE]
**područje region (area)**
**područje za piknik** picnic area
**podrum** basement
**poduzeće** company (business)
**pogreška** mistake
**pojačati** turn up (volume, heat)
**poklon** gift
**poklopac za objektiv** lens cap
**pokretne stepenice** escalator
**pokrivač** duvet
**pokvaren** faulty
**pokvariti** break (destroy)
**pokvariti (se)** break down (go wrong)
**pola** half
**polasci** departures (airport)
**polazak** depart (train, bus)
**policija** police
**policijska postaja** police station
**policijski izvještaj** police report
**poliester** polyester
**polijetati** leave (by plane)
**polupansion** bed and breakfast
**polje** field

**poljubac** *n* kiss
**poljubiti** *v* kiss
**pomoć** help
**poništiti** cancel
**ponoć** midnight
**ponoviti** repeat
**pop glazba** pop (music)
**popravak** *n* repair
**popravirti** *v* fix
**popraviti** *v* repair
**popuniti** fill out (a form)
**popust** discount
**porcija** portion
**poruka** message
**poruka** *n* text (phone)
**posao** business
**poseban** special
**posjeći (se)** *v* cut (wound)
**poslati** *v* post
**poslati** e-mail *v* e-mail
**poslije** after (time)
**poslije podne** p.m.
**poslijepodne** afternoon
**poslovan čovjek** businessman
**poslovni centar** business center
**poslovno** on business
**posluga** room service
**postolar** shoe repair
**posuditi** borrow
**pošta** *n* mail, post office
**poštanska markica** post stamp
**poštanski sandučić**
 mailbox [postbox BE]
**poštarina** postage
**potiljak** back (head)
**potok** stream
**potpisati** *v* sign
**potpuna usluga** full-service
**potraživanje od osiguranja**

insurance claim
**potres (mozga)** concussion
**potvrda** certificate
**potvrditi** confirm
**pouzdan** reliable
**povjesno mjesto** historic site
**povrat novca** refund
**povratna boca** returnable bottle
**povratna karta**
round-trip [return BE] ticket
**povremeno** occasionally
**poziv na račun primatelja poziva**
collect [reverse-charge BE] call
**pozivni broj** code (area, dialing)
**pozlaćen** gold plated
**poznati** popular (well-known)
**pozvati** invite
**požarni alarm** fire alarm
**požarni izlaz** fire door
**pramenovi** *n* highlights (hair)
**praonica** laundromat [launderette BE]
**praškast** powdery (snow)
**prati u perilici** machine washable
**pratiti** follow (pursue)
**pravac** direction
**pravi** real (genuine)
**pravo naprijed** straight ahead
**prazan** empty
**prečišćeni petrolej** kerosene
**predivan** magnificent
**predjelo** appetizer [starter BE]
**predložiti** suggest
**predmet** item (object)
**predstava** *n* play (theater)
**predstaviti se** introduce oneself
**pregled** examination (medical)
**pregrijati** overheat
**preko** across
**preko noći** overnight

**prekrasan** beautiful
**premješten** dislocated
**preplašen** frightened
**preporučena pošta** registered mail
**preporučiti** recommend
**preračunati se** *v* overcharge
**preseliti** *v* move (change of room)
**presjedati** change (bus, train)
**presvući** change (baby)
**pretinac za prtljagu** luggage locker
**pretjeran** outrageous
**prevesti** translate
**previše** too (extreme)
**prevoditelj** interpreter
**prezalogajnica** snack bar
**prezervativ** condom
**prezime** family name
**pribor za jelo** utensils
**pridružiti se** join (a group)
**prihvatiti** *v* accept
**prijatan** enjoyable
**prijatelj** friend
**prijaviti** declare
**prijavnica** registration form
**prije** before (time)
**prije podne** a.m.
**prijeći** *v* cross (street)
**prijevod** translation
**prikazati** *v* show
**priključak** extension (phone)
**prikolica** trailer
**prilog** side order
**primjer** example
**pripadati** belong
**priredba** *n* show (presentation)
**pristajati** fit
**pristup** access
**privlačan** attractive
**prizemlje** ground floor

**prljav** dirty
**proba** specimen
**probati** try
**procjep** *n* leak
**prodavač** shop assistant
**prodavaonica** store
**prodavaonica obuće** shoe store
**prodavaonica odjeće** clothing store
**prodavaonica pića**
   liquor store [off-licence BE]
**prodavaonica sportske opreme**
   sporting goods store
**prodavati** sell
**program** program
**program zabavnih događanja**
   entertainment guide
**prolaz** pass (place)
**proljeće** spring
**proljev** diarrhea
**promet** traffic
**prometni sat** rush hour
**prometni znak** road sign
**promijeniti** change (money)
**propisati** prescribe
**propustiti** miss (lack)
**prostirka** bedding
**prostor** space
**prostorija za sastanke** meeting room
**provesti** spend (time)
**provizija** commission
**prozirna kuhinjska folija**
   plastic wrap [cling film BE]
**prozor** window (house)
**prsa** chest (body)
**prsluk za spašavanje** life jacket
**prst** finger
**prsten** ring
**prtljaga** luggage [baggage BE]
**prva klasa** first class

**prvenstvo prolaza** right of way
**ptica** bird
**pub** pub
**pumpa** pump (gas station)
**pun** full
**puni pansion** full board
**puno** a lot
**pustiti** let go
**pušač** smoker
**pušiti** smoke
**putanja** route
**putnička agencija** travel agency
**putnički ček** traveler's check [cheque BE]
**putnik** passenger
**putokaz** sign post
**putovanje** journey
**putovanje brodom** boat trip
**putovati** *v* travel
**putovati s ruksakom** *v* backpack
**putovnica** passport

## R

**račun** bill (restaurant)
**računar** computer
**računovođa** accountant
**radijator** heater
**raditi** *v* work
**radno vrijeme** business hours
**rak** cancer (disease)
**rame** shoulder
**rani** *adj* early
**ranije** earlier
**rano** *adv* early
**raskrižje** intersection [junction BE]
**raspored** schedule [timetable BE]
**rastavljen** divorced
**ravan** *adj* level
**ravnatelj** director (company)
**razdoblje** period (time)
**razdvojen** separated

**razgledati** browse (shop)
**razglednica** postcard
**razgovarati** v talk
**razumjeti** understand
**ražanj** skewer
**rebro** rib
**recepcija** reception (desk)
**recepcionar** receptionist
**reciklaža** recycling
**reći** v say
**regenerator** conditioner
**registracija putnika** n check in
**registracijska oznaka auta**
    license plate number
**reket** racket (tennis, squash)
**remen** belt
**rendgen** X-ray
**rent-a-car** car rental [hire BE]
**restoran** restaurant
**reuma** rheumatism
**rezervacija** reservation
**rezervirati** v reserve
**rezervni** spare
**ribarnica** fish store [fishmonger BE]
**ribnjak** pond
**rijadak** rare (unusual)
**rijeka** river
**riva** sea front
**rječnik** dictionary
**robna ruća** department store
**rock glazba** rock (music)
**roditelji** parents
**rođak** cousin
**rođen** born
**rođendan** birthday
**rok trajanja** expiration date [expiry
    date BE]
**romaničan** romantic
**ronilačka oprema** diving equipment
**roniti** dive

**roštilj** barbecue
**ručak** lunch
**ručna prtljaga**
    carry-on [hand BE] luggage
**ručni mjenjač** manual transmission
**ručni vez** embroidery
**ručnik** towel
**ruka** arm (body part)
**rukav** sleeve
**rukavica** glove
**rukotvorine** handicrafts
**ruksak** n backpack
**ruševine** ruins
**ruž za usne** lipstick
**ružan** ugly

## S

**s podtitlom** subtitled
**sa zakašnjenjem** late (delayed)
**sada** now
**sadržiti** contain
**sam** alone
**samoposluživanje** self-service (gas
    station)
**samostan** monastery
**samozaposlen** self-employed
**sandala** sandal
**sapun** soap
**sastanak** appointment (business)
**sat** clock, hour
**satelitska televizija** satellite TV
**saten** satin
**sauna** sauna
**sedativ** sedative
**sef** n safe
**seks** sex
**semafor** traffic light
**sestra** sister
**sestrić** nephew (sister's son)
**sestrična** niece (sister's daughter)

**sezonska karta** season ticket
**sići** get off (bus, train)
**siguran** sure
**sigurnost** safety
**silovanje** *n* rape
**silovati** *v* rape
**simptom** symptom (illness)
**sin** son
**sinagoga** synagogue
**sinkroniziran** dubbed (movie)
**sintetičko vlakno** synthetic fiber
**siperak** bib
**sjajilo za usne** lipgloss
**sjećati se** remember
**sjedalo** car seat
**sjedalo do prozora** window seat
**Sjedinjene Američke Države (S.A.D.)**
    United States of America (U.S.)
**sjedište kraj prolaza** aisle seat
**sjena** shade
**sjesti** sit
**sjever** north
**skija** ski
**skijaška čizma** ski boot
**skijaški štap** ski pole
**skipass** lift pass (skiing)
**skladatelj** composer
**skoro** almost
**skratiti** *v* trim
**skrenuti** turn
**skup** expensive
**skupiti** collect
**skuter** scooter
**slabo varenje** indigestion
**sladak** sweet (taste)
**slamka** straw (drinking)
**slastičarnica** pastry shop
**slati** send
**slati poštu** *v* mail
**slavan** famous

**slavina** faucet [tap BE]
**sletjeti** *v* land
**slijediti** follow (road, sign)
**slijep** blind
**slika** painting
**slikar** painter
**slikati** paint
**slobodan** free (available)
**slomiti** break (a body part)
**slomljen** broken
**složiti se** agree
**slučajno** accidentally
**slušni aparat** hearing aid
**služba** service (religious)
**službeno odijelo** formal dress
**sljedeći** next
**smanjiti** turn down (volume, heat)
**smaragd** emerald
**smeće** garbage [rubbish BE]
**smiješan** funny
**snažan** strong (potent)
**snijeg** snow
**snimak** exposure (photos)
**sniženje** reduction (price)
**soba** room (hotel)
**solist** soloist
**soul glazba** soul (music)
**spa** spa
**spasavalac** lifeguard
**spavaća kola**
    sleeping car [sleeper wagon BE]
**spavaća soba** bedroom
**spavati** sleep
**specijalist** specialist
**spol** sex (gender)
**spomenik** monument
**spomenuti** mention
**spor** slow
**sporo** slowly
**sport** sport

**spreman** ready
**spužva** sponge
**srce** heart
**srčani udar** heart attack
**srebro** silver
**sreća** luck
**srednji** medium
**sredstvo protiv bolova** painkiller
**sredstvo za čišćenje** cleaning supply
**sredstvo za desinfekciju** sterilizing solution
**sredstvo za pranje posuđa** dishwashing liquid
**sresti** meet (appointment)
**sretan** happy
**sricati** *v* spell
**stadion** stadium
**stan** apartment
**stanica** stop (bus, tram)
**star** old
**stari grad** old town
**staviti** put
**stepenice** stairs
**stići** arrive (car, train)
**stijena** rock (land formation)
**stil** style
**stol** table
**stolica za hranjenje djece** highchair
**stopalo** foot
**stran** strange
**strana valuta** foreign currency
**stranka** party (social)
**strašan** terrific
**stric** uncle (father's brother)
**stroj** engine
**stroj za fotokopiranje** photocopier
**student** student
**studirati** *v* study
**stupanj** degree (temperature)
**sudoper** sink

**suknja** skirt
**suncobran** umbrella (sun)
**sunčane naočale** sunglasses
**sunčanica** sunstroke
**sunčano** sunny
**sunčati se** sunbathe
**super** superb
**supermarket** supermarket
**sušen** dried
**sutra** tomorrow
**suvenir** souvenir
**suvenirnica** souvenir store
**suvremeni ples** contemporary dance
**svađa** *n* fight
**svaki** every
**svaki dan** every day
**svaki sat** every hour
**svakodnevni** *adj* daily
**svetište** shrine
**sveučilište** university
**sviđati se** *v* like
**svila** silk
**svjestan** conscious (awake)
**svjetal** *adj* light (color)
**svjetlo** *n* light
**svjež** fresh
**svrbiti** itch
**svući se** undress oneself

## Š

**šah** chess
**šal** scarf
**šala** joke
**šalica** cup
**šalica za mjerenje** measuring cup
**šalter za prodaju karata** ticket office
**šalter za registriranje** check-in desk
**šampon** shampoo
**šansa** odds (betting)
**šator** tent

**šatorske štange** tent pole
**šešir** hat
**šetnja** *n* walk
**šibica** match (light)
**širok** loose
**šišanje** haircut
**šišati** *v* cut (hair)
**škare** scissors
**Škotska** Scotland
**škura** shutter (window)
**špilja** cave
**štake** crutches
**štednjak** stove [cooker BE]
**šuma** forest

## T

**tableta** pill (tablet)
**tableta za spavanje** sleeping pill
**taj** that
**tajnik** secretary
**također** also
**taksi** taxi
**taksi postaja** taxi stand [rank BE]
**taman** dark
**tamo** over there
**tampon** tampon
**tanak** thin
**tanjur** plate
**tapiserija** tapestry
**tava** frying pan
**tečaj** exchange rate
**tečaj jezika** language course
**tečaj mijenjanja novca** currency
    exchange rate
**tek** appetite
**telefon** *n* telephone
**telefonirati** call (telephone)
**telefonska govornica** telephone booth
**telefonska kartica** phone card
**telefonski broj** telephone number

**telefonski poziv** telephone call
**telefonski račun** telephone bill
**televizor** TV
**temperatura** temperature (body)
**ten** tan
**tenis** tennis
**tenisica** sneaker
**tenisko igralište** tennis court
**tepih** carpet
**terapija** course (medication)
**terasa** terrace
**teren za golf** golf course
**teretana** gym
**terminal** terminal
**termometar** thermometer
**termos-boca** thermos
**težak** hard (difficult)
**ti** those
**tih** quiet
**tijekom** during
**tipičan** typical
**tisak** *n* press
**tjedan** week
**toaletni papir** toilet paper
**točan** right (correct)
**točka** point
**toranj** tower
**torba** bag
**torbica** purse [handbag BE]
**tradicionalni** traditional
**trafika** tobacconist
**trajati** *v* last
**trajekt** ferry
**tramvaj** tram
**tranzit** transit (travel)
**traper** denim
**traperice** jeans
**trava** grass
**tražiti** ask (request)

**trbuh** stomach
**trebati** v need
**trenutak** moment
**trg** square (town)
**trgovački centar**
  shopping mall [centre BE]
**trgovaonica zdrave hrane**
  health food store
**trgovina mješovite robe** produce
  [grocery BE] store
**trošiti** spend (money)
**trudna** pregnant
**tržnica** market (marketplace)
**tumač** translator
**tumor** tumor
**tunel** tunnel
**tura s vodičem** guided tour
**turist** tourist
**turističke atrakcije** sights
**turistički ured** tourist office
**turpija za nokte** nail file
**tuš** shower
**tvrd** tough (food)

**U**

**u** at (time, place), on (day)
**u živo** live
**ublizini** nearby
**ubod insekta** insect bite
**ubod komarca** mosquito bite
**ubrus** napkin
**učitelj** teacher
**učiti** learn (language)
**udar** shock (electric)
**uganut** sprained
**uganuti** v twist (hurt)
**ugasiti** turn off
**ugodan** friendly (place, atmosphere)
**ugriz** n bite
**uho** ear

**uhvatiti** catch (bus)
**ujak** uncle (mother's brother)
**Ujedinjeno Kraljevstvo**
  United Kingdom (U.K.)
**ujutro** morning (time)
**ukazati** indicate
**ukraden** stolen
**ukrcati (se)** to board; embark
**ukusan** delicious
**ulaz za invalidska kolica**
  wheelchair ramp
**ulaznica** admission charge
**ulica** street
**ulje** oil
**umirovljenik** senior citizen
**umjesto** instead
**umjetnička galerija** art gallery
**umjetnik** artist
**umoran** tired
**unajmiti** v hire
**uniforma** uniform
**unutra** inside
**upala** inflammation
**upala pluća** pneumonia
**upaliti** turn on
**upaljač** n lighter
**uplašen** afraid
**upoznati** meet (get to know)
**upravitelj** manager
**uputa** instruction
**uputiti** v direct (to a place)
**uračunat** included
**ured** office (place)
**urezati** engrave
**usisavač vacuum cleaner**
**usko** adv tight
**uskoro** soon
**usluga** service (in restaurant)
**usna** lip
**usta** mouth

**utakmica** game (sports)
**utičnica** plug
**utopiti (se)** drown
**uvećati** enlarge (photos)
**uvijek** always
**uvozni** imported
**uzak** narrow
**uzeti** take (carry)
**uzeti lijek** take (medicine)
**uživati** enjoy

**V**

**vadičep** corkscrew
**vaditi** extract (tooth)
**vagon** car (train)
**vagon-restoran** dining car
**valuta** currency
**vani** outside
**vanjski** external
**vatra** fire
**vatrogasci** fire department [brigade BE]
**večer** evening
**večera** dinner
**večeras** tonight
**večernja haljina** evening dress
**već** already
**veći** bigger
**vegetarijanac** n vegetarian
**veličanstveno** stunning
**veličina** size
**velik** big
**ventilator** fan (electric)
**veslanje** rowing
**veza** connection (train)
**vidikovac** overlook [viewpoint BE]
**vidjeti** see (observe, witness)
**vikend** weekend
**vilica** fork
**vinograd** vineyard
**vinska karta** wine list

**visina** height
**visok** high
**višak prtljage** excess luggage
**više** more
**vječnica** town hall
**vjera** religion
**vješalica** coat hanger
**vlak** train
**vlasnik** owner
**vlastiti** adj own
**voda** water
**vodič** guide (tour)
**voditi** v lead
**vodokotlić** flush
**vodopad** waterfall
**vodoskok** fountain
**vođa grupe** group leader
**voljeti** v love
**vozač** driver (car)
**vozačka dozvola** driver's license
**voziti** drive
**vrat** neck (body)
**vrata** door
**vratiti** return (restore)
**vratiti se** come back (return)
**vrč** carafe
**vreća za spavanje** sleepingbag
**vrećica za povraćanje** air-sickness bag
**vrećice za smeće**
  garbage [rubbish BE] bags
**vremenska prognoza** weather forecast
**vrh** peak
**vrijednost** value
**vrijeme** time
**vrsta** type (sort)
**vrt** garden
**vrtoglavica** dizziness
**vruć** hot
**vruća voda** hot water

**vrućica** fever
**vučna služba** tow [breakdown BE] truck
**vuna** wool

## Z

**za** in (period of time)
**za** for (time)
**za pušače** smoking (room)
**zabava** fun
**zabavni park** theme park
**zaboraviti** forget
**začepljenje** constipation
**začinjen** spicy
**zadnja svjetla** rear lights
**zadnji** *adj* last (previous)
**zadovoljstvo** pleasure
**zagrijati** *v* warm
**zagrliti** *v* hug
**zahod** toilet
**zahtijevati** require
**zahtjev za odštetu** claim check
**zahvaliti se** *v* thank
**zainteresiran** interested
**zakazana posjeta** appointment (doctor)
**zaključati** *v* lock
**zakuska** snack
**zamijeniti** exchange
**zamjena** *n* replacement
**zamjenski dio** replacement part
**zamoliti** *v* please
**zamrzivač** freezer
**zanimanje** profession
**zanimljiv** interesting
**zarazan** contagious
**zaražen** infected
**zaručen** engaged
**zaručnica** fiancée
**zaručnik** fiancé
**zastoj u prometu** traffic jam

**zastor** curtain
**zatvor** prison
**zatvoren** close (store)
**zatvoreni bazen** indoor pool
**zatvoriti** *v* shut
**zaustaviti (se)** *v* stop
**zauzet** busy
**zavoj** bandage
**završiti** *v* end
**zdjela** bowl
**zdravlje** health
**zdravstveno osiguranje** health insurance
**zemlja** ground (earth)
**zemljopisna karta** map
**zglob** joint (body)
**zgodan** pretty
**zgrada** building
**zgrada parlamenta** parliament building
**ziherica** safety pin
**zlatarnica** jeweler
**zlato** gold
**znak** *n* sign
**znamenitost** attraction (monument)
**znati** know
**zora** dawn
**zračna kompanija** airline
**zračna luka** airport
**zračna pošta** airmail
**zrcalo** mirror
**zub** tooth
**zubar** dentist
**zubna kapica** cap (dental)
**zubna kruna** crown (dental)
**zubna proteza** denture
**zubni konac** dental floss
**zubobolja** toothache

## Ž

**žalostan** sorry
**žarulja** lightbulb
**žedan** thirsty
**željeznički kolodvor**
  train [railway BE] station
**željezo** *n* iron
**ženski** female
**živac** nerve

**živjeli** cheers (toast)
**životinja** animal
**žlica** spoon
**žlica za mjerenje**
  measuring spoon
**žlijezda** gland
**žohar** cockroach
**žulj** blister
**žurba** rush